New Nations and Peoples

The Philippines

The Philippines

RAYMOND NELSON

with 36 illustrations and 3 maps

1968

WALKER AND COMPANY
NEW YORK

To Corazon

Library of Congress Catalog Card Number: 66-22509

First published in the United States of America in 1968 by Walker and Company, a division of the Walker Publishing Company, Inc.

Printed in Great Britain by Billing and Sons Ltd, Guildford

Contents

5

Preface

THE PHILIPPINES occupies a rather unique place in Southeast Asia. Comprising a chain of some 7,000 islands stretching for nearly one thousand miles from Formosa to Borneo in a tropical area of vast economic potential and beauty, these islands contain some of the richest mineral deposits, forests, fisheries and potential sources of hydro-electrical power in the world. Though geographically the Philippines is considered a part of the Malayan world, it is unique in being the only predominantly Christian country in Asia and the third largest English-speaking country in the world. Reputedly it is the first country in Southeast Asia where an armed nationalist movement was generated to fight against a colonial power, first Spain and then the United States.

The peoples of the islands are basically Mongoloids and have a Malay culture, made stronger and more mature by the transfusion of a variety of foreign blood notably from India, China, Japan, Arabia, Spain and America. Naturally the long period of Spanish rule between 1565 and 1898 has left indelible traces on the culture of the Filipinos. The Spaniards introduced Catholicism which supplanted the spread of Islam except in the southernmost islands of the archipelago. They built churches and constructed the earliest centres of education, such as the University of Sto. Tomas; they introduced the theatre, encouraged the development of sculpture and painting, and of course brought with them the stimulation of Latin American and European culture. When the United States took over the Philippines in 1898, there were a large number of Filipinos with mixed Spanish blood who formed the major part of the upper class, and helped the Americans establish their form of colonial government. However, the policy adopted was one of social and economic progress in contrast to the record of the Spaniards. Emphasis was placed on the development of health and educational services, and English was introduced in the schools. The participation of Filipinos in the government paved the way to national independence after the Japanese occupation during the Second World War.

With the elimination of colonial rule, after a period of nearly four hundred years, the Philippines became an independent republic in a ceremony on 4 July 1946, celebrated by thousands of cheering Filipinos and witnessed in war-ravaged Manila by the representatives of twenty-seven nations. Today the Philippines take its place among the nations of the world with a government modelled on that of the United States and a belief in free enterprise and economy.

When writing about a nation it is easy to forget that the people of the country perhaps look at life and the world through eyes different from our own. Only after spending a considerable amount of time among the people, things which at first seemed strange and exotic become normal. Many of my comments about Filipino life do not, therefore, depend on what others have observed but come from my own experiences in this country, during a period of revolutionary change and transformation.

Despite the devastation of the Second World War, the Filipinos have shown that they have the capacity, if encouraged, to build and maintain a democratic country. Even if there are inequalities in Filipino society, and the newspaper headlines emphasize smuggling, crime, corruption in the government, and the widening gap between the wealthy and the poor, it is well to remember that similar headlines appear in the newspapers and magazines of most democratic countries. Just twenty years after the inauguration of the Republic, the Philippines has a pattern of self government which, even if not perfect, is a model of stability among the troubled and insecure countries of Southeast Asia.

1   The islands and their people

THE PHILIPPINES, the oldest ex-colonial country in Southeast Asia, is an archipelago of 7,100 islands stretching for nearly 1,000 miles between the southern tip of Formosa and the northern parts of Borneo and Indonesia. The archipelago has a breadth of 700 miles, is bounded on the east by the Pacific Ocean and in the west by the South China Sea. It thus occupies a strategic position in relation to Vietnam and the Chinese mainland. The Philippines has a total land area of 115,707 square miles, is smaller than Japan, approximately the size of Arizona, and slightly larger than the United Kingdom. The coastline is irregular and extends for a distance of 10,850 miles, about twice the length of the coastline of the United States. Among the many natural harbours, Manila Bay, with a circumference of 120 miles, is one of the finest in the world.[1]

The actual number of islands in the archipelago, of which fewer than 1,000 are inhabited, varies from time to time as new isles are created by volcanic action or others slowly submerge into the sea. Most of the large islands have palm-lined shores and are covered with a variety of rock formations, steaming swamps, jungles, green rice fields, interspersed with sprawling towns and villages built of bamboo and the nipa palm. In early geological times it is probable that some of the islands were connected by land bridges with Borneo and Malaya; and the Philippines may have extended to Formosa and as far as Australia via the Celebes, the Moluccas and the southernmost islands. Discoveries of crude stone tools and the remains of animals now extinct in these islands, like the elephant, support the belief that direct contact with the mainland of Asia existed in the distant past. Much of the vegetation and orchid flora plainly show signs of

9

Indo-Malayan origins, while forms of plant life found only in the northern districts of Luzon, the biggest island, provide evidence of a former connection with Formosa.

The islands are also links in the great volcanic and coral chains of Southeast Asia which run from Indonesia and Borneo towards Japan, and are characterized in the Philippines by a backbone of towering mountains running from north to south. A number of the mountain peaks range to heights of up to 9,800 feet, their ruggedness contrasting sharply with the rich green lower slopes and coastal plains suited to agriculture. The country is dotted with volcanoes, mostly dormant, though at least ten are still active. Among these may be mentioned Mt Mayon in Albay Province, famed for having an almost perfect cone, and Mt Taal situated about thirty-five miles south of Manila, the largest city in the Philippines. This volcano, which is in the centre of Lake Taal, is the smallest known to man, but nevertheless, when it erupted again in September 1965 severe damage and loss of life was caused to nearby villages.

Large lakes with an abundance of fish are found in interior regions, and many swamp lands bordering the sea have been ingeniously developed by the local people as fish ponds or laid out as sea-water beds to obtain salt by solar evaporation. Mangroves grow profusely along parts of the low-lying coastlands and, looking like a forest supported on stilts in the soft mud and brackish water, make a vivid contrast to the spongy moss, lichens and ferns covering higher ground. In areas of dense population the mangrove swamps are systematically exploited to provide firewood, charcoal and material for building. Tannin is obtained from the bark. The leaves of the deep-rooted Nipa palm are particularly favoured for roofing huts as they do not decay when dried. The palm sap is collected and prepared as a drink; when distilled it is used as vinegar. Other species of palm include the coconut, so important to the economy, betel, and the climbers *Daemonorops* and *Calamus* which yield rattan cane.

The forests and lower slopes of the islands have a diversity of flora almost without parallel elsewhere in the world, yielding, for example, the fruit of the distinctive fig tree, the bark of the cinnamon, gutta-percha, resins and gums. Prominent among the tropical trees and huge grasses are the banana, abaca, eucalyptus and last but not least the bamboo which has played such an important part in the lives of Asian peoples.

Thousands of flowering plants have been identified in the Philippines, many of which are valuable for medicinal purposes. A few of the names include bougainvillea, cannas, fire trees, hibiscus, jade-vine, jasmine, periwinkle, poinsettias, white ginger and the sweet-scented sampaguita, which is nowadays cultivated as the national flower of the Philippines. Numerous varieties of orchids are indigenous, the most famous, known all over the world, is the *Vanda Sanderiana* or Waling Waling.

Fruits are abundant, and the mango is the queen of them all; native fruits include anonas, atis, breadfruit, calamansi, dayap, guava, jackfruit, papaya, star apple and tamarind. Bananas, important as a food crop to the early Filipinos, are cultivated in many varieties. Banana leaves are often used for wrapping and, in rural areas, as plates. A favourite fruit is the avocado pear, others that deserve mention are the chicos with a flavour like a date, lanzones, mangosteens, Mindanao grapefruit and pomelo. Pineapples, thought to have been introduced by the Spanish, are cultivated mostly for export.

In the midst of such a rich and diverse flora it is disconcerting to find that almost a quarter of the Philippines is covered by a savanna type of vegetation, usually cogon, which may grow to heights exceeding 4-6 feet. These rank grasses, or coganales, have spread mostly as the result of the controversial system of shifting cultivation known in the Philippine archipelago as 'caingin' farming in which an area of forest is cleared by burning to increase the fertility for additional cropping. Natural restoration of the cleared area takes a long time and usually results in the spread of savanna. Much valuable timber is destroyed. Once an area is covered by cogon grass, which has very dense and strong roots, it is practically impossible to recultivate.

Nearness to the equator gives the Philippines a monsoon climate, particularly in its western regions, while typhoons occur in the north and east. Throughout the year it is warm, humid and cumulatively enervating to most people from temperate climates. There are three seasons, hot-dry from March to May, hot-rainy from June to the end of October, and cool-dry, beginning in November and lasting until some time in March. The end of the hot-dry season is usually marked by violent thunderstorms and torrential rains. As the islands are surrounded and washed by warm seas, the air temperature ranges between 60-90°F, with a mean temperature of 80°F over the year; variations are thus far less than on the mainland of Asia. Climatic differences when they occur are mainly caused by rainfall and more noticeable from west to east than from north to south. In fact, drought is a perennial problem in many districts, especially during April and May, when the lateness of the monsoon or frequent breaks in the rains jeopardize the growing period of various crops such as rice and sugar-cane. In the Ilocos regions of Luzon drought can occur for periods of three to five months. From these parts down through central Luzon and as far south as the island of Mindanao and the Zamboanga peninsula one can trace a definite dry season. In contrast, the winter monsoon brings heavy rain to the east coast when the wind is in a northeasterly direction. After the start of the southwestern monsoon, usually some time between the end of July and the beginning of September, the rains become torrential and not only are many roads made impassable but bridges and dikes are washed out. Typhoons, called locally 'bagyo', increase in frequency and strength during these months and often cause considerable damage.[2]

However, despite frequent droughts there is a wide distribution of primary forest, and from the mountainous districts of northern Luzon down to the southernmost islands of the Philippine archipelago more than 40 per cent of the land is heavily forested. Tropical hardwoods are present in large numbers, the Dipterocarps with their straight white trunks rising to heights exceeding 75 feet before fanning out at the top in an umbrella of foliage. Much of the best timber has hitherto been inaccessible, but recently more than 25 million acres have been classed as commercial forests.

The fauna of the Philippines is almost as diverse as the flora and has attracted the attention of naturalists from many countries who have endeavoured to define some sort of boundary between Asian

12

and Australian forms. Though large animals such as the elephant, rhinoceros and tiger no longer roam the archipelago, much of the existing animal life has clearly Asiatic origins, giving support to the conclusions reached by the British naturalist, A. R. Wallace, who saw a definite boundary line running north and south from points east of Java and Borneo. This line extended from the Macassar Strait to the eastern coast of the Philippines.[3]

Among animals to be found today is a wild buffalo called the tamaraw which is restricted to Mindoro. It is a fierce beast and cannot be domesticated like its cousin, the carabao, the work-horse of the Philippines and the mainstay of the Filipino farmer. Wild pigs, deer and monkeys are found in many regions. A remarkable monkey-like creature is the tarsier, which is somewhat smaller than a squirrel, a distinctive feature being its enormous goggle-like eyes. Monkeys have become a commercial commodity and large numbers are exported for scientific research.

The climate is ideal for many kinds of reptiles and amphibians. There are about 100 species of lizards and one, the iguana, resembles a small cayman. Large broad-snouted caymans inhabit many of the lakes, and numerous crocodiles live in rivers, swamps and pools of brackish water. Of the crocodiles the Estuarine is the most dangerous and one of the largest, growing to more than 12 feet in length. Normally long-lived, it is now faced with the threat of extinction at the hands of hunters who find it profitable to sell the skins for leather goods. Snakes abound in the islands and include giant boa-constrictors and pythons. Remote regions, especially in the mountainous districts of Mindanao, are populated by huge bats. Many measure five to six feet across their wings. The dried excrement called guano is often collected by the natives and used as fertilizer, being rich in nitrogen and phosphates.

The insect life of the archipelago follows closely the pattern found in Malaysia and Indonesia and is one of the most varied in the world. Butterflies of brilliant colours, strange forms and diverse size are found in great profusion. This wealth of species is even more evident in the bird population ranging from tiny wrens to the monkey-eating eagle, and in the incredible richness of the marine fauna with thousands of different kinds of fish from giant sharks to the tiny goby, barely half an inch long, found in Manila Bay. Besides the many varieties of edible and pearl oysters, corals, sponges and water turtles, there are several species of terrapins which are highly valued for food. The Hawksbill, the smallest of the water turtles, has a special economic worth, being the source of commercial tortoiseshell. Crabs are abundant, and one of the most remarkable is the popularly named Robber Crab which climbs coconut palms. With its two powerful claws it snips the stem of the nut and husks the fruit. Among the countless molluscs, both land and aquatic, may be mentioned the large clam *Tridacna gigas*, which often attains a weight of 500 lb. and length of about four feet, and *Conus Gloria Maris*, Glory of the Sea, of which the shell is considered by experts to be the rarest and most valuable.

Of the very large number of islands belonging to the Philippines only 462 are a square mile or more in area. Only 2,773 have names and the eleven largest occupy some 95 per cent of the total land area. These eleven islands can be classified in three geographic divisions: first, Luzon, Mindoro and their adjoining islands; second, the Visayas including Cebu, Leyte, Panay, Negros, Samar, Masbate and Bohol; third, Mindanao and the Sulu archipelago together with Palawan and its adjacent islands to the west.

The principal islands are traversed by rivers which are often navigable, and constitute a rich potential source of hydro-electric power. The most important rivers are the Cagayan, Agno, Pampanga, Pasig, and Bikol in Luzon, and the Rio Grande de Mindanao and the Agusan in Mindanao.

The most important island is Luzon in the north with an area of 40,814 square miles. Here are situated some of the major cities of the Philippines. Manila, centre of politics and government administration, adjoining Quezon City, the new capital now rapidly expanding and the home of the University of the Philippines, and Baguio, the mountain resort. Much of Luzon is mountainous, and a number of peaks rise above 6,600 feet, the highest being Mt. Pulog in the Eastern Cordillera, reaching a height of 9,600 feet. The longest mountain range is the Sierra Madre which runs from Cagayan down the east coast to Sorsogon in the south. Southern Luzon is characterized by numerous coastal indentations and deep gulfs, illustrating the manner of the break-up of the land mass and the variety of geological formations and relief typical of the islands of the Philippines, as seen especially in the many small isles scattered over the mediterranean sea separating Luzon from Mindoro. Mindoro is high and very mountainous with regions of forests and swamps. It is to a large extent undeveloped and wild.

The Visayas, southeast of Mindoro, are a group of seven islands of differing shape of which Cebu is the hub. The water separating the islands is generally shallow. Between Leyte and Samar, as well as Panay and Negros, the depth is less than 100 feet, whereas the Tañon Strait dividing Negros Oriental and Cebu is nearly 2,000 feet deep. In general, the structure is that of narrow coastal plains or hills and mountains extending right down to the sea. Where the plains have broadened out, for instance in northwest Negros, former volcanic activity has left an enriched soil which has contributed to the cultivation of sugar-cane. Cebu is the capital of the province of the same name and is the oldest city in the Philippines. After Manila it is probably the busiest city in the archipelago.

Mindanao, which is next to Luzon in size with an area of 36,906 square miles, has a very uneven coastline with deep bays and inlets. While Mindanao presents contrasts of structure it does not have the same ridges or mountainous characteristics as Luzon. Narrow coastal plains almost encompass the island, broadening out near Davao and Pagadian. The Agusan valley in the northeast has extensive forests, although the middle part is a region of scattered lakes, swamps and creeks. Farther west and southwest is the valley of the Rio Grande de Mindanao. Between Agusan and Cotabato are the provinces of Bukidon and Lanao with broad level plains and a rolling terrain girded by mountains. Mindanao is still developing and has enormous potential wealth. Its largest cities, such as Davao and Zamboanga, are becoming increasingly important as trading centres.

Beyond Zamboanga is the Sulu archipelago consisting of a large number of small islands clustered between Mindanao and the northeast tip of Borneo. Many of these islands consist only of coral and volcanic matter but Jolo, the main island, though irregular in shape, is characterized by rich tropical vegetation and extinct volcanoes. Northwest of the Sulu archipelago is the elongated island of Palawan, formerly called Paraqua, which runs unbroken for nearly 250 miles with an average width of 18 miles. It is one of the most remote provinces of the Philippines, consisting mainly of a mountainous ridge with a coastline fringed with coral and rocky caverns. Palawan has recently come into the limelight as a result of the findings of Philippine archaeologists. In caves facing the China Sea they have found Stone Age tools and pottery, together with a fossil skull-cap estimated to be at least 15,000 years old.

In terms of population the Philippines is one of the fastest-growing countries in the world, four-fifths of the people living in the rural areas. Since the emergence of the country as an independent nation, attention has been focused on the implications of this growth. From the beginning of the Spanish occupation in the sixteenth century to the take-over by the Americans in 1898 the population increased slowly from an estimated 500,000 to 7·5 million. By 1939 the number had increased to 16 million. After 1948 the population increased rapidly, and by 1960, when the last census was taken, the figure had reached 27 million representing an annual growth rate of 3 per cent. At this rate the present population will more than double in the next 25 years. Such an increase is impressive but it does not necessarily mean that the Philippines will become overcrowded. Problems will be rather those of maldistribution than of overall congestion. One finds, for instance, about 20 persons per square mile in Palawan compared to 150-400 persons per square mile in northeastern Mindanao and Luzon. Localized areas of great density include the provinces of Rizal and Laguna with densities at the present time of between 1,000 and 2,000 persons per square mile. The case of Manila is somewhat different as the city has a density exceeding 80,000 persons per square mile.[4]

It is well to remember, however, that the vital statistics of the Philippines are grossly defective. Deficiencies of the present civil registration system are many; these are due to lack of transportation and communications facilities, tribal locations and the common habit of many people among the non-Christian minorities not to register births and deaths. Thus it is difficult to assess accurately whether a similar annual population growth of 3 per cent has taken place among the two million Filipinos who make up the minority groups.

Altogether there are more than seventy native dialects, apportioned among regions, provinces and tribes. Of these only eleven may be considered major ones and include Tagalog, spoken in Manila and many of the central provinces of Luzon; Sugbuanon, spoken in Cebu and parts of Mindanao; Hiligaynon, spoken in Negros Occidental and Iloilo; Samarnon, spoken in Samar and Leyte; and Ilocano, spoken in several parts of northwest Luzon. At present the official languages are English, Spanish and Pilipino, known before 1962 as Tagalog, which is being used more and more in official circles. Spanish is of course a survival of the colonial era, and is the language of much Filipino literature. The majority of the people have Spanish names. During the American régime English became the language of the constitution, law, education and commerce, and is still widely used throughout the archipelago.

Who are the Filipinos? Are they an Asiatic people? There is no definite answer to such questions. They are a hospitable and Western-oriented people who, except for minor tribes, are basically Mongoloid with a Malay culture modified by centuries of contact with Chinese, Japanese, Hindus, Arabs, Spaniards and most recently Americans. Though the country is geographically in Asia, one should not be surprised to find a beautiful stone church with a baroque façade in a tropical setting or a smiling individual with Chinese features and a Spanish name conducting business in an American way. Seldom in other parts of the East does one come across such a blend of Oriental and Occidental cultures. In mountainous regions scattered through the islands small Negroid people are still found who live mainly by the bow and arrow or blowgun. Other tribes are found in mountain regions north of Manila whose

B

way of life has scarcely changed since the Stone Age, while in the islands of Mindanao and Sulu there are Muslim tribes whose culture vividly displays the grandeur achieved before the Spanish conquest in the sixteenth century. In Manila, which has an estimated population of some two million, largely made up of Filipinos, Chinese, Americans, Europeans and other nationals, one sees the impact of the twentieth century — concrete skyscrapers and palatial villas which contrast pointedly with slums worse than New York's Harlem. In this centre of all political, economic and cultural activity in the Western sense, Filipino commuters cram themselves into gaudily decorated buses and war-surplus jeeps of American origin, or they sit patiently in sleek limousines waiting for an opening in the congested traffic. In a quiet side-street, reminiscent of Spain, people jog by in high-wheeled horse-drawn calesas or Spanish gigs.

It was from Manila that the Spaniards in the sixteenth century consolidated their conquest of the archipelago and spread the Catholic faith. It was also in Manila that the Americans displaced the Spaniards at the turn of the nineteenth century, fought Filipino nationalism and gave impetus to Western ideas and technology. It was here during the Second World War that the Japanese inaugurated the first Republic of the Philippines and in 1946 that the returning Americans fulfilled their pledge to grant Filipino independence and inaugurated the present Republic. Although neighbouring Quezon City is the official capital, Manila still retains its importance as the administrative and traditional capital of the Philippines. Manila not only nourished the nationalistic intelligentsia of the nineteenth century but was a focal point for the first movement in Southeast Asia to take arms against a colonial power.[5]

More than 90 per cent of the Filipinos are Catholic, a constant reminder of the long period of Spanish colonization. About 4 per cent are Muslims, and there are some Protestants; the remainder are pagans. To know and understand the modern Filipino one must nevertheless be acquainted with his still living past and with those of his fellow countrymen, sometimes called the colourful minorities, who have chosen to retain cultures so different from the one adopted by the majority. The Muslims, sometimes called Moros — to their

18

resentment — are widely known as a fierce, brave and independent minority who follow the Islamic system of laws, social conventions and marriage ceremonies. Various tribes have successfully resisted all attempts by Spanish and American colonizers, including some of their fellow Filipinos, to subdue and Christianize them. Though Philippine law does not recognize divorce, among the Muslims and indigenous religious groups it is allowed. The Muslims live by their own code according to which the Datu (chieftain) or Sultan is the constituted ruler and judge. The Philippine government has accepted the Muslim regions as special areas, and provincial officials from Manila work closely with the Datus and the agama courts which adminster Islamic law.

Hitherto, the policies of the central government have not removed feelings of distrust among the Muslims who feel that they are not only misrepresented but a forgotten minority. Many of the Datus and Sultans try to counter this feeling, but one major obstacle is the Philippine educational system. Students, many of whom recite the Koran in Arabic, make repeated accusations that college history books give a false picture of the Muslims, while some popular songs and dramas are resented as attacks on their culture. Consequently, many Muslims refuse to send their children to school.

The second largest minority group live in the high mountain valleys of north-central Luzon and are commonly called Igorots. This is in origin a deprecatory term meaning 'mountain people' first used by the Spaniards. The name Igorot is as much resented as the word 'Moro' by this proud and sometimes recalcitrant people who belong to a composite Malay-Indonesian stock. Numbering altogether nearly half a million, they are a virile, hard-working people who in earlier days were notorious for tribal warfare and headhunting. They have preserved their identity, customs and folklore since long before the Christian era, and all attempts by the Spaniards to impose their rule failed. In this mountainous region are the world's oldest rice terraces still in use. Those in the Hungduan area and between Bontoc and Banaue, including Sagada, being particularly impressive with terraces extending from the floor of the valley to heights exceeding 3,000 feet. These terraces were constructed

19

by arduously levelling off section after section of the mountainside and using stone retaining walls. Successive generations have added one level after another, water being brought by a system of channels and dams.

Many prominent men have emerged from the different tribes and found a place in various professions. While most of the older people still retain their tribal beliefs and religions, many of the younger generation have been converted to Christianity. Despite the establishment of a Commission on National Integration in 1957 to bring about the moral, material, social, economic and political advancement of the non-Christian minorities, and despite the establishment of social centres and farm settlements, there is a general tendency to ignore the claims of the different tribes to retain their cultures. This may stem from the old Spanish concept that native culture does not exist and that tribal traditions are nothing more than forms of paganism. There seems to be a general apathy to the enormous problems of integration, not made easier by the number of dialects.[6]

One of the most debated minorities are the Chinese though their numbers, estimated at about 300,000, are probably lower than in any other major state in Southeast Asia. Regarded by both the Spaniards and Americans as aliens and made to suffer many restrictions, they have also been considered by Filipinos with a sort of mixed fear and jealousy. This is mostly due to their skill as traders and financiers but also to the illegal entry of many Chinese into the country, despite the reduction of the immigration quotas. Another irritation has been the fact that many Chinese who have become Filipinos by length of stay, or who have intermarried, have not given up their Chinese way of life. This exclusiveness has caused a feeling of both envy and animosity among many Filipinos who are convinced that the Chinese cannot be trusted, a feeling kept alive by the Chinese passion for organization, whether it be in the home or in business.

The *mestizos*, the Spanish name for people of mixed Spanish-native parentage and now used to denote people of mixed race, have never been classed as a separate community. In the Philippines the mixture of racial characteristics often produce combinations seldom seen in Asia of a fine aquiline nose wedded to high cheek bones, a light skin colour with an inexplicable slant in the eyes! These are some of the features of the mestizos who constitute a considerable portion of the wealthy and educated class. From them have come many prominent figures in public life and science. This dependence upon such an élite is an important difference between the Philippines and neighbouring territories. While the mestizo, known sometimes as the *cacique*, are now less of a dominant social and landowning class, they still play an influential and important part in the commercial and political development of the Republic.

2   Early history

THE EARLY HISTORY of the Philippine archipelago is fragmentary though sufficient to indicate that during the thousands of years that preceded the arrival of the Spaniards in the sixteenth century continuous change took place in the human and political geography of the islands and surrounding countries, as a result of the migration of peoples and the dissemination of new ideas and cultures.

It is thought that ancient man first came to the Philippines from China and the Malayan archipelago, some 250,000 years ago during the Middle Pleistocene or Ice Age, when the advance and retreat of vast glaciers in the northern hemisphere affected regions near the Equator. Advancing ice-packs lowered water levels in the seas and rivers. Land areas between China, Malaysia and the Philippines, now separated by water, were then probably connected by land bridges which allowed the migration of men and animals. Man during this age had no agriculture and relied on food gathering and hunting.

Although fossil remains of Pleistocene man have not been found in the Philippines, the bones of extinct animals have survived. Among the fossils have been found the remains of large and small elephants, wild buffalos, rhinoceroses, deer, pigs and the stegodon. It is probable that the early hominids of the islands were near kinsfolk to both Peking man (Sinanthropus pekinensis) and Java man (Pithecanthropus erectus), It is significant that a fossil skull-cap recently discovered in a cave in Palawan has characteristics dating back to the late Pleistocene. Although the pattern of migration is diffused, it is reasonable to assume that the peopling of the archipelago occurred before the post-glacial rise in sea-level submerged the land bridges. Among these people were pygmy Negritos who are thought to have arrived from central Asia some 25,000 years ago and others, probably Mongoloids, who may have brought with them tools made of

22

sharp flakes of flint, agate and tektite glass usually in the form of saws, scrapers, knives and engraving points. Many examples of these 'Microlithic' tools have been uncovered in Luzon and are similar to discoveries made in Mongolia. The available evidence would suggest that the people were food gatherers, fishermen and hunters like the earlier Palaeolithic people. Some came from south China, others from the Tonkinese mainland and some from the south via Borneo.[7]

As the land bridges disappeared the surrounding seas became the highways that led to the Philippines, and the Neolithic peoples who followed were experienced sailors. They possessed an advanced culture and brought the first knowledge of agriculture to the islands. During a period of some 1,500 years covering the transition from the Middle Neolithic to the Late Neolithic many changes took place in the design of tools and implements. New techniques such as sawing and drilling made their appearance.

Jade or nephrite, probably brought by Late Neolithic people from south China and Indo-China, also began to be extensively used for fashioning highly valued ornaments and implements. This Late Neolithic period may be dated as beginning some 2,000 years ago and lasted until the first century of the Christian era. Homes were then built of stone with grass-covered round roofs, and more and more innovations in agriculture were introduced including the cultivation of grains and rice. Extensive use was made of the system of shifting cultivation, a system which is practised in many parts of the Philippines to this day. During this time much of the cultural influence came from the mainland of Asia, but contrary to the belief of many it is considered possible that some migrating people came from the Pacific islands, where seamanship and navigational practices had been highly developed.

A large movement of people to the Philippine archipelago occurred around 200 BC and continued until the beginning of European colonization. Known generally as Malays, they first began to penetrate from western Indonesia via Borneo, the Sulu archipelago and Palawan to the coastal regions of the Visayas, Mindanao, Mindoro and southern Luzon. The Malays brought with them their

Iron Age tools, a knowledge of smelting and forging iron, glass-making, new techniques of weaving such as tie-and-dye, and the use of the back-loom, a type still found in Mindanao and the Mountain Province, Luzon. It is believed that the Malays had had extensive contacts with India, China and Arabia before migrating to the Philippines. They had their own laws, language and a rudimentary alphabet which laid the foundation for much of the pre-Spanish folklore in the Philippines. By this time bronze and copper implements and weapons were in use, although stone was still the primary material, and the peoples of the islands had begun to develop and extend the system of irrigated rice cultivation by paddies with dikes to collect and store water.[8]

As a result of these migratory influences and a blending of the Negrito, Indonesian and Malay cultures, a new civilization began to emerge in the Philippines, probably during the fifth century. There was knowledge of numbers, and writing was done by engraving on bark or by using a sharp point dipped in the sap of jungle plants to write on banana or other palm leaves. Religion consisted mostly of the worship of ancestral and nature spirits and the use of charms to protect a person from illness and malign spirits. Megaliths were erected to the memory of dead chiefs; and mediums, usually women, practised divination. Headhunting was common in certain regions. Such animistic beliefs and practices are still part of the lives of many present-day Filipinos, even if they should profess to be Christian or Muslim.[9]

During this part of the Christian era, Indian and Arab traders began to appear more frequently in the Philippines, as trade between China, India and the rest of the Malay archipelago increased. Trade was further stimulated in the ninth century when Arab traders, barred from the central China coast, discovered an alternative route starting from Malacca and passing through Borneo, the Philippines and Formosa. The competing cultures of India, China and the Middle East brought about marked changes in the economic and social life of the coastal towns of the Philippines. The Chinese, Indian and Middle Eastern merchants found abundant food in the Philippines, with plenty of rice, bananas, yams, millet and gabi;

vegetables such as patola, kondol, beans and eggplant. Fishing, from both the open sea and inland waters became an important industry. Crude industries came into being, such as mining, metallurgy, lumbering and clothmaking. Gold and coins were introduced as an instrument of exchange in addition to barter. Towards the end of the tenth century the Arab traders were allowed to re-enter the Chinese ports of Chuan-Chow and Canton, resulting in an increase in trade between China, Borneo and the Sulu archipelago. Trade between the Philippines and Borneo brought more far-reaching cultural influences from the powerful Malay Kingdom of Sri Vijaya on Sumatra. By AD 1180, Sri Vijaya's rule embraced much of Indonesia, Borneo, and parts of the Malay peninsula. During the twelfth century the Arab traders found themselves with strong competition from the Chinese. Officially China had mixed feelings about foreign trade, even though it brought prosperity to large numbers of people and the treasury was enriched by the import duties levied. Ideologically trade could not be supported because of the Confucian theory that it was something sordid and inferior. Nevertheless, the desire of China to play an influential part in trade won the battle of conscience. At the close of the thirteenth century the Arabs had more or less withdrawn from trade in the area.[10]

Significant changes now began to take place in the surrounding countries. Siam was emerging as the most powerful state of the Indo-Chinese peninsula and coincident with this the Ming Dynasty decided to restore the loss of Chinese prestige by extending Chinese influence. Ming China found in the Malay ruler of the newly established kingdom of Malacca, which paid tribute to Siam, a willing and loyal servant. Encouraged by Chinese support, Malacca broke off allegiance to Siam and gradually gained control of adjacent territories. Chinese armies were despatched to re-occupy the Annamite lands and seven expeditions were sent out during the period 1405–1433, a major event in Chinese history. Commanded by the court eunuch Cheng Ho, some of these expeditions, on voyages to the Malay archipelago, passed through the Philippines and stopped at Lingayen, Manila, Mindoro and Sulu. According to the ancient *History of the Ming Dynasty* recorded by Chang Ting-Yu,

China appointed a resident Governor during the fourteenth and fifteenth centuries who exacted tribute and exercised nominal rule over the Philippines.[11]

The main influence of China on the Philippines would appear to be economic rather than cultural, although the use of gongs and silver was introduced, as were new techniques in metallurgy and craftmanship. A large number of present-day customs such as ancestor worship, filial respect for parents and arranged marriages are clearly of Chinese origin. Items of dress, including the sleeved jacket and loose trousers for women, are still in vogue among sections of the Chinese and Muslim population in the archipelago.

As a result of Chinese backing, Malacca developed trade with Indian and Middle Eastern Muslim merchants. The acceptance by the Malaccan ruler of the Islamic faith and the spread of Muslim doctrines throughout the peninsula brought significant changes to Southeast Asia. Associated with trade, the new religion spread across Malaya. The introduction of Islam to the Philippines, at about the same time, by Malay immigrants and visiting traders did not at first change the old beliefs of the majority of peoples, who continued to worship ancestral spirits.

Towards the end of the fifteenth century the Chinese stopped sending expeditions to the Philippines and Malayan archipelagos; and by this time Spain and Portugal had become keen rivals in colonizing new lands. After the line of demarcation had been established by Pope Alexander VI in 1493, Spain and Portugal signed the treaty of Tordesillas, which reaffirmed the papal decision to divide the world into two spheres of influence but moved the line a further 800 miles west enabling Portugal to claim Brazil and Spain the Philippine Islands.

The discovery by Diaz de Novaes, in 1488, of the Cape of Good Hope route to the East, gave the opportunity to the Portuguese to outflank the Muslim states and this secure control of the lucrative spice trade. In this way they could strike at the economic roots of Islamic strength and simultaneously carry the Christian crusade a stage further. By 1510, Portugal had established maritime supremacy in the Indian Ocean and, Goa became the capital of the Portuguese

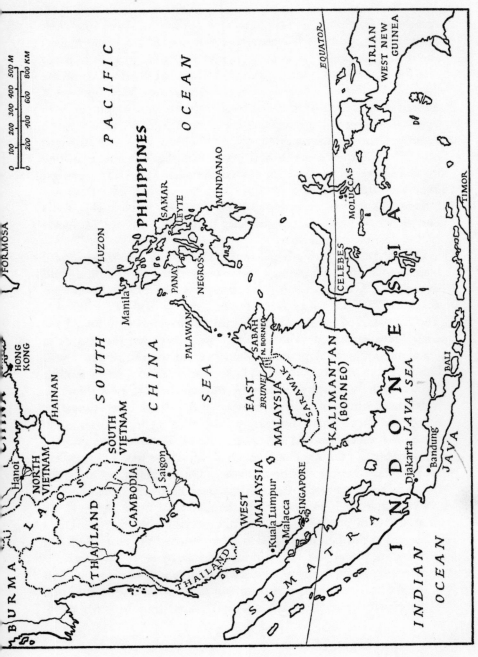

Map of the Philippines in Southeast Asia

empire in the East. The way was now open to Malacca, the chief
spice market, which fell after heavy fighting between the Malays
and d'Albuquerque's forces in 1511. Present at the taking of Malacca
was the Portuguese captain Ferdinand Magellan, destined to be the
discoverer of the Philippines. Several years later Magellan found
himself disfavoured by the Portuguese throne and sought exile in
Spain. At Saragossa, he was presented to Charles V, to whom he
promised the complete discovery of the Moluccas and adjacent
islands by a distinct route from the west. His plan was further helped
by the intense rivalry which existed between Spain and Portugal
over the discoveries of Columbus and the growth of Portuguese
influence in the East. Spain saw an opportunity to exploit Magellan's
knowledge, secure a part of the spice trade and bring the Moluccas
within the Spanish sphere.

On 10 August 1519 Magellan and his fleet of five ships set sail
from Seville on the first stage of a voyage that was to be long and
hazardous. Accompanying Magellan was the Venetian knight,
Antonio Pigafetta, who has left the best record of the expedition.[12]
The fleet arrived off Brazil at the end of November, followed the
coast southwards and explored the regions between the Rio de la
Plata and southern Argentina. Magellan had to wait nearly a year
before finding the channel which linked the Atlantic with the Pacific.
Undeterred by mutiny, treachery and the loss of two ships, he
began his crossing of the vast expanse of the Pacific, a crossing that
lasted for more than three months before sighting Guam. He
continued westwards and sighted the mountains of southern Samar
on 17 March 1521, and on the small adjoining islands, Magellan
met for the first time Philippine natives. On the island of Limasawa,
he made his first blood-pact with the local chieftain, Kolambu.

According to Pigafetta, when the hour for mass arrived, we
landed with our body armour, but carrying our other arms, and
dressed in our best clothes. Before we reached the shore with our
boats, six pieces were discharged as a sign of peace. We went in
marching order to the place consecrated, which was not far from
the shore. Two kings, Kolambu and his brother Siagu, embraced
the captain-general—Magellan—and placed him between them.

The two kings were sprinkled with musk water. The mass was offered up. The kings went forward to kiss the cross as we did but did not offer the sacrifice.

After the Mass a large wooden cross was erected on the summit of a hill overlooking the sea, as Magellan solemnly took possession of the land in the name of Spain, naming it the archipelago of St. Lazarus. After a short stay Magellan, accompanied by Kolambu, continued his voyage to Cebu and landed there on 7 April. The importance of Cebu as a trade centre was immediately obvious to the Spaniards, and Magellan made another blood-pact with chief Humabon. Again this was followed by a Mass and the planting of a wooden cross. On the same day a large number of Filipinos including the wife of Humabon, were converted to Christianity.

After dinner the priest and some of the others went ashore to baptize the queen, who came with fifty women. We conducted her to the platform and she was made to sit down upon a cushion. She was shown an image of our Lady, a very beautiful wooden child Jesus, and a cross. Thereupon she was overcome with contrition, and asked for baptism amid her tears. We named her Johanna, after the emperor's mother.

After the baptism Magellan gave her an image of the child Jesus, which can be seen today in Cebu City.[13]

Humabon, as well as other chieftains, had been impressed by the Spanish ships and armour. However, Lapu-Lapu, chieftain of Mactan, a small island protecting the port of Cebu did not accept the superiority of the white men. Magellan was annoyed by this challenge to Spanish might, and with a force of some fifty Spaniards and a large number of newly-won Cebuan allies, he landed on Mactan, 27 April. The fighting strength and courage of Lapu-Lapu and his men had been underestimated, and in the ensuing battle Magellan was killed and his men routed. The defeat changed the allegiance of Humabon and other Cebuans. Four days later the Filipinos attacked and massacred a number of Spanish officers and men, though a few Spaniards managed to set sail for Tidore. Magellan's mistake thus cost him his life and Spain the allegiance of the local people; but Magellan's plan to reach the Moluccas had succeeded and the knowledge gained from the voyage had been shared with the other officers. One ship, the *Victoria*, commanded by Del Cano, left Tidore loaded with spices and returned to Spain on 6 September 1522. The world had been circumnavigated, and the way paved for the Spanish colonization of the Philippines.

In 1542 the name of the archipelago was changed to Islas Filipinas in honour of Philip II of Spain. However, little was achieved until an expedition commanded by Miguel Lopez de Legazpi conquered Cebu in 1565. With him was his cousin, Andres de Urdaneta at the head of the first Augustinian mission. A Spanish settlement was established and eventually became the present Cebu City. Legazpi adopted a policy of persuasion and religious conversion to obtain the support of the people. If the friars failed by peaceful means to win allegiance, then force would be used. Returning to Mexico, Urdaneta discovered that the track of the westerlies between the latitudes 31° and 44°N made possible a reliable trade route from the Philippines to New Spain in addition to Magellan's more southerly route. This discovery convinced the Spanish that the Philippines could be linked with their interests in Mexico.[14]

Though Portuguese ships endeavoured to blockade the settlement in Cebu, by 1569 both Cebu and Panay were controlled by Spain. Aided by the missionaries and using force only where necessary, Legazpi was able to pacify the local inhabitants. With Cebu and Panay as bases the Spaniards successfully extended their rule to the other islands.

In 1570 Legazpi, sent a force commanded by his grandson Juan de Salcedo to Luzon to attack the Muslim stronghold, now known as Manila. After bitter fighting, it was conquered but it was not until 24 June 1571 that Legazpi proclaimed Manila the capital of the Philippines and became the first governor of the archipelago. Subordinate to the Spanish Viceroy in Mexico City, he organized both the military conquest and the civil administration. Valuable support was received from the missionaries who were eager to increase the number of converts to the Catholic faith. Islam's hold was too weak to resist the zeal of these early missionaries, who met little resistance from the people in the northern and central areas.

Accustomed to the worship of ancestral spirits, the Filipinos quickly adopted the rites, forms and ceremonies of the strange new religion expounded by the friars. Nevertheless in Sulu, Mindanao and Palawan the story was otherwise. Here the Mohammedan faith was strongly embedded and provided the ideological and political basis necessary to unite the Datus and the Sultanate of Sulu in a common cause against the Spaniards.

Legazpi concentrated on consolidating the Spanish position in Manila and Cebu and laid the foundation for the future unification of many of the island communities. On 20 August 1572 he died, having successfully brought under the sovereignty of Spain a great part of what today constitutes the Philippines. Although faced with hostility from the natives, the Spaniards had achieved control of vital coastal areas. Apart from sporadic attacks, including an attempted invasion by a Chinese pirate in 1574, the task of consolidation was carried out with little bloodshed. Much of the Spanish success was a result of the untiring efforts of the missionaries in winning the confidence of the Filipinos, especially the women. The Spaniards found in Manila a number of Chinese merchants, Japanese and a few of mixed race. The majority of the people, called Indians by the Spanish, had an olive complexion, flat noses, large eyes and long hair. They were considered indolent and not trustworthy.

Trade was encouraged and expanded in the early years of Spanish rule. Chinese and Japanese junks came regularly to the islands, bringing a variety of goods such as salted meats, pots and bowls, gunpowder, writing cases and silk. Many of the visiting traders were accompanied by skilled craftsmen, weavers, painters, tailors and shoemakers. The Japanese, among other things, taught the local people the technique of breeding ducks and fish by scientific methods which greatly impressed the Spaniards.

Nevertheless the Spanish authorities in Manila began to view with suspicion the increasing number of Chinese immigrants. From about 150 Chinese in 1571, the number had risen to some 6,000 in 1581. To discourage them, special license fees and poll taxes were levied, and the Chinese were restricted to a special district just outside the city walls within range of Spanish cannons. 'The Spaniards endeavoured rigorously to limit the number of Chinese who were envied and hated for their industry, frugality, and cunning. They were an abomination, moreover, in the eyes of the priests as being irreclaimable heathens, who presented a bad example to the natives; and the government authorities feared them because of their being loyal subjects of so powerful a nation'.[16] Although clashes had occurred earlier between Japanese immigrants and Spanish forces, by 1600 Japanese immigrants were fewer than the Chinese and better treated.

After the conquest of Manila, plans had been conceived by the conquistadores and missionaries to bring both China and Japan within the Spanish empire in the East. These schemes found little support in the Mother Country, preoccupied with European wars and the annexation of Portugal. The union of Portugal and Spain between 1580 and 1640 resulted in Philip II discouraging all activities that might lead to a clash between the two countries. However the Spaniards in Manila knew that Portugal had been successful in establishing beneficial relations with Japan and this only increased their covetousness. A peculiar situation had also arisen in the Catholic world. In 1585 the Pope had acknowledged the position of the Portuguese in Japan, and ordered that they, alone, should be allowed to carry on trading and missionary activities. The great Catholic power of the century, however, was Spain, though one of the conditions of the union of 1580 had been that Portugal would continue to administer her overseas possessions and would have exclusive control of missionary activity in the Far East. The Spanish authorities in Manila ignored this ruling and in 1593 sent a party of friars to Japan as ambassadors from the governor of the Philippines. It was stressed that they had come neither to trade or to indulge in religious activity. Nevertheless, within a short time the friars had founded a church at Kyoto and a convent in Osaka. This immediately led to intense rivalry between the Spanish and Portuguese in Japan and may be said to have caused the Japanese reaction which resulted in all foreigners and Christians being expelled from the country.

The Spanish occupation of the Philippines and the plying of galleons between Manila and Acapulco in Mexico encouraged many traders, particularly the Chinese, to build up a flourishing trade in fine silks, porcelain, spices and perfumes, paid for with Mexican silver. Only the Muslim port of Jolo in the Sulu archipelago had at this time attained a comparable position in foreign trade. The galleons were owned by the Spanish crown and operated according to a procedure known as the Laws of the Indies. Each galleon was divided into compartments to hold cargo. Tickets, called *boletas*, corresponding to the number of compartments available, were distributed to officials, including religious orders and Spanish residents. Ticket holders were entitled to a share in the profits arising from each voyage. This system encouraged both fraud and corruption. Many ticket holders found it more profitable to sell their shares to merchants at inflated prices. In the forefront as bankers were the charitable foundations, called Obras Pias, who were backed by Catholic fraternities.

Oriental goods, especially silks, transported by the galleons found a ready market in the Spanish-American colonies and competed with Spanish-made merchandise to such an extent that in 1583 merchants of Seville secured the issue of a royal decree ordering the cessation of Chinese trade with New Spain. The Viceroy of Mexico, to whom the decree was forwarded, would not put it into force, arguing that the commerce of the Philippines was absolutely necessary to Mexico.

During this time the Spanish were often faced with local uprisings following acts of oppression. Little headway was made against the Muslims who were constantly engaged in raiding and plundering in the southern islands. Because of the commercial importance of Sulu and Borneo, the Spaniards in their determination to stamp out the Muslim faith sent expeditions to Jolo and Brunei in 1578. These were initially successful in curbing local inhabitants but aroused resentment in the Muslims. Growing opposition compelled the Spaniards to send further expeditions, but these were too small to conquer the Muslim strongholds completely. The compaigns provoked bitter hostilities and started a bloody conflict that dragged on over a period of three hundred years.

The mutual jealousy and distrust of the Spaniards and Portuguese in Japan had by 1592 made the Shogun, Toyotomi Hideyoshi, suspicious of the *namban-jin* or Europeans. An increasing fear of

Spanish imperialism strengthened his resolve to take the Philippines unless a tribute was paid. His demand was conveyed to the governor, Gomez Perez Dasmarinas, in Manila, who replied by sending an ambassador to Hideyoshi with gifts and a message which diplomatically evaded the demand for tribute, In view of Spanish plans to conquer the Muslims it was necessary to forestall any Japanese move against the archipelago. Further gifts were sent to Hideyoshi easing the situation until 1596, when the wreck of a galleon off the Japanese coast aroused old fears. Tensions between Manila and Japan had almost reached breaking point when Hideyoshi died in 1598. He was succeeded by Tokugawa Ieyasu, and during the next few years relations between the new Shogun and Manila improved.[17]

Restricting the Chinese to their own quarter in Manila did not reduce the growing hostility against the Spanish authorities, who often were guilty of harsh treatment. Fear gave way to a simmering hate and culminated in the first Chinese revolt in 1603. Artillery fire from the walls of Manila eventually dispersed the Chinese after much bloodshed. Survivors retreated to San Pablo, Laguna, where they suffered severe losses at the hands of Spanish forces. Similar outbreaks occurred in 1639 and 1662. During this time relations between the Spaniards in Manila and the Japanese Shogun had once again deteriorated. The Spanish friars had persisted with their religious activity and revived Japanese suspicions. The persecution of Japanese Christians was intensified and resulted in increased emigration to the Philippines. This continued until the Shogun stopped all contact between Japan and the outside world in 1639.

The system of civil administration, introduced by Legazpi, did much to unify many of the island communities. The governor-general exercised great power and was president of the *audiencia* or supreme court, the highest tribunal for civil and criminal cases. Outlying districts were ruled by *corregidores*, usually army officers, and *alcaldes* or mayors. *Caciquism*, or rule by one man or a family, was part of this system and widespread in Spanish America. This fitted well into the native system of rule by Datus and traditional chiefs. The Spaniards were well aware that the control of a new colony could not be fully accomplished without the assistance of

34

local rulers, and the Datus were allowed to continue, often being appointed as *gobernadorcillos* or petty governors. Though deprived of some of his former power, the Datu was allowed exemption from the payment of tribute and could compel the people to submit to forced labour for his personal requirements. The gobernadorcillo served also as mayor and municipal judge. The influence of the clergy was considerable, and the gobernadorcillos were careful to obtain their approval before issuing an official order. The end of the seventeenth century saw the emergence of a feudal class consisting of the descendants of the territorial rulers, many of whom had married Spaniards, and provided a necessary link between the mass of the people and the higher authorities.

Gradually revolts against the colonial administration became more frequent because of the harsh treatment and abuse meted out by local officials, the imposition of a tribute and forced labour, despite a royal decree of Philip II abolishing slavery. The tribute payable to the Spaniards consisted of a sum of money or kind. Full tribute was payable by a family with children; unmarried men and women paid one-half tribute. In general the economy followed the pattern of the Americas. Large tracts of land, including villages and resources, were granted to the Catholic church and to loyal Spanish officials. Known as the *encomienda* system, it was a new name for the *repartimiento* awards which had been instituted by Hernan Cortes in Mexico. The holder of the *encomienda* was called *encomendero*.

The introduction of this encomienda system soon reduced the mass of Filipinos to the level of serfs. Forced labour, called *polo* had to be rendered by all men, young and old, for a period lasting one to two months. Wealthy Filipinos were allowed exemption by paying a sum of money called *falla*.

It was the class and social division between the large landowners and privileged officials on the one hand and the common people, mostly poor tenant farmers, on the other, which constituted—to some extent still constitutes—the threat to internal stability in the Philippines. During 333 years of Spanish occupation the Filipinos rose in more than one hundred revolts. The Frenchman Pierre Sonnerat in 1806 wrote:

The people, therefore, who have submitted to the Spanish yoke, scarcely exhibit any traits of a polished nation. Indolence, a dereliction of life and timidity constitute their character, and misery is their habitual state . . . people who have escaped from the yoke by removing themselves to places where the Spaniards cannot attack them . . . they nourish in the extremity of their asylum an implacable hatred against the strangers, whom they consider as the oppressors of their native land . . . they incessantly meditate on, and prepare the means of revenge . . .[18]

The Filipino revolts failed owing to a lack of unity, leadership and organization, but their actions should have served as a warning to the Spaniards of the need for reform. Apart from the fervent efforts of the friars, the initiative shown by the early colonizers was giving way to a lackadaisical inertness. The eighteenth century saw the beginning of a gradual decline of Spanish power in Southeast Asia.

3   The decline of Spanish control

AFTER THE original Augustinian friars, it was the missionary effort of the Jesuits. Dominicans and Franciscans that became dominant in the Philippines, their zeal and enthusiasm being paralleled by the encomendero, who usually prepared the way by supressing local hostility and resistance and obtaining the support of the ruling chiefs. Since the local inhabitants did not have a powerfully organized religion, it was not difficult to convert them to Catholicism, and within a decade after 1571 some 200,000 converts had been made. By 1898 there was an estimated total of six million Catholics out of a population of some seven million.

During their long occupation, the Spaniards did little to promote economic development, having become more or less dependent on the galleon trade. Chinese immigration was allowed to continue, as they were too useful to be kept out, serving and managing the retail trade as they did. The majority of the population, or 'Indios' as they were then called by the Spaniards, were with few exceptions a source for providing food and servants under the watchful eye of the church and local authorities. Profits from the sale of merchandise in the Americas, mostly Chinese in origin, sustained the easy life and culture of the day for the favoured few. Gone was the conviction that had led many of the early conquistadores and missionaries to see their role as Christian crusaders liberating a people from pagan practices. Forgotten also was the intention to replace the friars by parish priests as a part of community development. The friars did not relish losing their power or lands, and although the civil authorities began to come more into conflict with the church over the use of available resources, and sought to reduce the participation

37

of the clergy in local administration, the friars and missionary orders exploited their landed estates and more often than not, in the role of *hacendero*, committed many abuses. Among the numerous peasant revolts, mention can be made of the unsuccessful uprisings during the years 1745–56, when Tagalogs from many towns, including Nasugbu, Hagonoy, Parañaque, Silang and Cavite, fought for the restoration of communal land which had been taken over by the missionaries for cattle raising.

Though the Spaniards were able to suppress these unco-ordinated revolts, little was done to remove the cause for unrest. The Spanish attitude, in general, was one of indifference and apathy—an attitude, however, that was soon shaken by events taking place in Europe. Towards the end of the Seven Years' War, which had enabled England to lay the foundations of its empire in the East, France was facing defeat and sought Spanish naval assistance. A secret alliance known as the 'family compact' was concluded between the French and Spanish thrones in 1761 and resulted in the outbreak of war between Spain and England at the beginning of 1762. British forces, following success against the French in America, were available for attacks against the Spanish colonies; and from India, the surrender of Pondicherry permitted other forces to be sent as an expedition to the Philippines under the combined command of Admiral Samuel Cornish and General William Draper. Towards the end of September 1762 the British fleet, consisting of seven ships of the line and four smaller vessels, entered Manila Bay, creating consternation and confusion in the capital. Despite inadequate defences a call to surrender was ignored by the temporary governor-general, Archbishop Manuel Rojo, acting on the advice of civilian advisers, and the short siege of the city began. On 5 October, British forces, which included impressed French soldiers and Indian sepoys, broke through the defences and forced the garrison to capitulate. Though the Spaniards agreed to pay a war indemnity of some millions of dollars it did not prevent a period of pillage and destruction which lasted for nearly two days.

In anticipation of surrender the Spanish leaders had earlier empowered a judge of the royal audiencia, Simon de Anda, to carry on the struggle if necessary in some other part of the archipelago. Leaving Manila on the eve of its capture, he established his head-quarters and the seat of Spanish government at Bacolor, a town some forty miles north of the capital. Almost simultaneously with the British capture of Manila, unco-ordinated revolts broke out against Spanish rule in a number of provinces but with the assistance of the clergy, caciques and large sums of money, Anda was able to organize sufficient forces to suppress and check any signs of unrest among the people. Though Anda quickly formed an army which harassed the British during their occupation, it did not openly challenge them. The British forces, on the other hand, were too few to carry on a campaign in the provinces and restricted operations to an occasional foray.

Following the end of the Seven Years' War and the signing of the Treaty of Paris in February 1763, Spain lost a large part of its territory in America and ceded Florida to England in return for Havana. England, however, restored the Philippines to Spain. Archbishop Rojo died at the beginning of 1764, and the British allowed Anda and his forces to enter Manila on 31 May of that year. Later the British forces were withdrawn to India. Though the occupation had not lasted for more than twenty months the British had restored the Sultan of Sulu, Alimud Din, to his throne, following his imprisonment by the Spaniards for treason. In return they received parts of North Borneo, including the island of Balambangan.

Spanish prestige had fallen to a low level, and the shock of the near loss of the colony was a signal for Charles III to authorize the new governor, Francisco Torre, to repair Manila and carry out necessary reforms. The first efforts were against the power of the economically dominant missionary orders, to augment revenue by means of better administration and the promotion of commercial prosperity. Charles III was determined to apply the principles of government which had been evolved by the Bourbon monarchy in France, and to subordinate the Church to the Crown. In particular he suspected the Jesuits of political intrigue, and in 1767 he decreed their expulsion from the American colonies, which included the Philippines. Anda, who had remained in Manila after the British withdrawal and then returned to Spain, was appointed governor-general in 1770 and, with the full support and authority of the Spanish king, launched a general attack on the position of the friars. He charged them with interference in civil affairs, neglect of their spiritual duties and opposition to the teaching of the Spanish language to the common people. The quarrel became bitter, but despite the backing of the Archbishop of Manila for the secularizing of land holdings, such reforms had little chance of success against the power exercised by vested interests. Efforts to curb the wealth and influence of the regular orders petered out after the death of Anda in 1776.[20]

In 1778 another governor-general, José Basco, arrived in the Philippines with the policy of making the islands self-sufficient and economically independent of Mexico. Steps were taken to improve the cultivation of cotton, sugar-cane, hemp and tobacco, and added impetus was given by the founding in 1781 of the Economic Society of Friends of the Country which provided economic services and popularized improved methods of agriculture. Though the society declined after Basco's return to Spain in 1787, it continued in operation more or less until 1898. During this period the first agricultural school was established in 1861.

Basco also created a government monopoly of tobacco growing. Certain areas, notably in Luzon, were instructed to raise tobacco, according to strict quotas, for purchase by the monopoly. Other government monopolies followed in quick succession, such as wines, gunpowder and the organization of cockfights, etc. During the next hundred years the islands became the greatest tobacco-growing country in the East. Enormous profits were realized by the government, but little went to the cultivators and producers. In the end corruption and administrative abuse, together with the consequent encouragement of smuggling, forced the abolition of the monopoly.

Reforms carried out by Charles III resulted in a loosening of the rigid controls imposed on trade among the colonies. Expanding economic activity facilitated the influx and spread of liberal ideas from Europe. In 1785, Charles III established the Royal Company of the Philippines to promote direct trade with Spain and with other

40

countries of the Orient, and to encourage Philippine agriculture and industry. Capital was provided by wealthy residents, Spanish bankers and commercial interests, both in Spain and Cuba, added to which was a one-eighth investment by the Spanish throne. Privileges were granted, such as the right to purchase supplies from government stores at special prices, exemption from customs duties and the use of the Spanish naval flag by its vessels. The company introduced foreign capital into the Philippines and succeeded initially in promoting the cultivation of cotton, sugar-cane and spices, and establishing textile factories. The company's business began to fail as a result of inefficient administration and competition from the galleon trade, which had been carried on by private merchants following the abolition of the government monopoly in 1815. The company was finally abolished by royal decree in 1834.

By the end of the eighteenth century Spain was faced with growing unrest in the American colonies. Already there was rivalry between the United States and England over the emancipation of the Latin American countries. After Napoleon's invasion of Spain in 1808, and the rise of liberalism, which revived a new Cortes and accorded the Philippines limited representation for the first time, Ferdinand VII, who had been restored to the throne, abolished the Constitution of 1812. He suppressed the Cortes and imposed a reactionary and despotic régime upon the Spanish people. In 1820 a military revolt at Cadiz, in protest against a force being sent to the colonies to crush rebellion, developed into a situation in which Ferdinand was compelled to capitulate. During this time Mexico, inspired by events in Europe, had revolted against Spain, achieving its independence in 1821 and bringing to an end its administrative control over the Philippines, exercised since the days of Legazpi. This resulted in Manila's looking towards Europe and a gradual relaxation of trade restrictions. With the opening of the Suez Canal, foreign commercial interests increased. More and more Filipinos, mostly the children of an emerging middle class, went to Spain and attended European universities, where they came into contact with the new ideals of liberalism. It was this group, influenced by events in Europe and the Americas, which provided the nucleus of the first nationalist movement to discuss publicly the failure of Spain to carry out the promises of reforms in government and religion. The influx of more European friars to take over favoured parish assignments had increased the discontent of the native clergy and added fuel to the smouldering political unrest.

After the Spanish revolution of 1868, liberal ideas of government spread to Manila in the wake of a new governor-general, De la Torre, who encouraged open discussion and aspirations for reforms, recognized the freedom of the press and introduced a more tolerant and humane policy of administration. However, within two years, with the restoration of the monarchy in Spain, De la Torre was replaced by General Rafael de Izquierdo, who reinstated a reactionary administration, banning political rights and resorting once again to repression and censorship of the press. Nevertheless, discontent about the cancellation of exemptions from rendering tribute and personal services, which workers in the naval arsenal at Cavite had long enjoyed, led to a mutiny by both Filipino troops and workers in 1872. Though the mutiny was local and quickly suppressed, the incident was utilized by the Spanish authorities to justify the arrest and punishment of many Filipino intellectuals whose actions and demands during the liberal governorship of De la Torre had rendered them undesirable to those now in power. Many were deported to the Marianas islands, others executed, including three Filipino priests, Fathers Burgos, Gomez and Zamora, who were charged with sedition, though their guilt was never established.

The harsh and arbitrary treatment meted out to those arrested determined the direction and life of a small group of young Filipinos in Europe and in the Philippines, who were banded together in a common cause to work for independence through their writings. Among these were, to mention a few; Lopez Jaena, the founder of the periodical *La Solidardad*, printed in Barcelona, which focused the attention of the Spanish liberals on the need for reform in the Philippines; Marcelo H. del Pilar; Mariano Ponce; the Luna brothers; Jose Ma. Panganiban; Dominador Gomez; Pedro A. Paterno; Eduardo de Lete; Antonio Ma. Regidor; and the most gifted of Filipino polemicists, José Rizal.

42

Rizal was born in Calamba, Luzon, on 19 June 1861, the son of a middle-class landowner and the seventh of eleven children; he received his early education at the hands of the Jesuits and Dominicans. A precocious student, influenced by his mother and imbued with nationalistic feelings promoted by a secret society of students, he left the Philippines in 1882 to travel and complete his studies in Europe. He emerged within a few years not only as a talented doctor, linguist, sculptor, novelist and propagandist but as a symbol of Filipino equality with the Spaniard. His first novel *Noli me Tangere* was published in Berlin in 1887. It exposed the evils of Spanish rule as well as the faults of his fellow-countrymen and the exploitation of Filipinos by Chinese traders; it aroused a storm of accusations from the friars and the authorities in the Philippines. Though proscribed in the archipelago, copies of the novel circulated secretly and were widely distributed. Rizal returned to the Philippines in 1887 but was compelled to leave again after some months because of threats to his safety. He returned to Europe and poured out a series of brilliant articles for *La Solidaridad*. His second novel, entitled *El Filibusterismo* ('The Rebellion') was, published in Belgium towards the end of 1891. Dedicated to the memory of the executed priests Burgos, Gomez and Zamora, this novel was clearly separatist and crystallized the nationalist movement in the islands. Many copies of *El Filibusterismo* were confiscated by Spanish customs officials in the Philippines. Following its publication and the subsequent persecution of his parents, who lived in the Philippines, Rizal decided to return to the archipelago. Along the way he stopped in Hong Kong, where he conceived the idea of establishing a Filipino colony in North Borneo. With his friend, Jose Basa, exiled in Hong Kong following the Cavite incident, he formed an association of Filipinos in the archipelago to be called the Liga Filipina.[21]

Towards the middle of 1892 Rizal decided to return to Manila, though he knew that he would be risking his life. He visited the new governor-general, Eulogio Despujol, and pleaded successfully for the pardon of his family. Official sanction to establish a colony in Borneo was, however, refused, and Rizal was asked not to engage in subversive activity. Well aware that he was under suspicion and being watched, Rizal spent the next few days with friends visiting the surrounding districts and quietly outlining his proposals for the Liga Filipina. These were based on the constitution written in Hong Kong and with the following aims:

1 Union of the Philippines into a compact, vigorous and homogeneous body
2 Provision of mutual protection in every difficulty and necessity
3 Defence against violence and injustice
4 Encouragement of education, agriculture and commerce
5 Carrying out the study and application of reforms.

On 3 July the Liga Filipina was founded in Manila at a gathering of close associates and friends which included Ambrosio Salvador, Deodato Arellano, Andres Bonifacio, Apolinario Mabini and Doroteo Ongjunco. This was a daring challenge to the Spanish authorities, and not surprisingly Rizal was arrested four days later and exiled to Dapitan. The arrest of Rizal meant to many the end of of the peaceful campaign for reforms and the need to prepare for armed struggle. On the day of his arrest a meeting was held among his associates who, impatient at the turn of events, supported the proposals of the radical Andres Bonifacio to organize a secret revolutionary society to carry out the ideas of Rizal, unite all Filipinos, fight for independence, and force the overthrow of the Spanish régime. Formally known as the *Katipunan ng mga Anak ng Bayan* ('Respected association of the sons of the people'), the society slowly recruited members and elected as the first president Deodato Arellano, the brother-in-law of M. H. del Pilar.

While these events were taking place, the Spaniards had been unsuccessful in their attempts to conquer the Sulu Sultanate. No Spanish general had recognized occupation as an essential factor in the pacification of Sulu until the well-planned campaign of the governor-general, Admiral José Malcampo. A peace treaty was signed with Sultan Jamalul Alam in 1878 recognizing Sulu as a protectorate and respecting Sulu customs, laws and religion. Spanish control over foreign relations was, however, declared indisputable. Earlier agreements made by the Sultan, ceding possessions in Borneo to the British North Borneo Company, were opposed at first but following a treaty with England and Germany in 1885, Spain relinquished all claims to Bornean territory, formerly ruled by the Sultans of Sulu.[22] Eventually the combined strength and unity of Sulu was reduced to small separate areas, but each retained sufficient tenacity to resist Spanish domination.

Events abroad were to have repercussions in the Philippines. From the 1850s onwards a large part of Spanish America had undergone an economic transformation as a result of British and North American investments. The Monroe Doctrine, propounded by the United States President in 1823, was intended to counter European influence in the American continent. British prestige in Latin America was seriously challenged. United States' intervention in the region became more forceful and turned in the direction of Cuba, which, like the Philippines, had experienced unsuccessful revolt against Spanish rule. Like the Philippines, Cuba had its revolutionary movement; one of its leaders, José Marti, successfully enlisted United States' support in the fight for freedom, many in the United States taking it for granted that after the island had been liberated from Spanish rule it would become a United States' dependency. Commercial interests were looking for profitable enterprises in which to invest money, and Cuba had the advantage of a sugar industry, cheap labour and a strategic position in the event of the construction of the Panama Canal. United States' relations with Spain were allowed to deteriorate, while Marti unified the independence movement through the Cuban Revolutionary Party, founded in the United States in the same year as the Katipunan in Manila.

By 1896, the Katipunan had grown to considerable size and included Emilio Jacinto, who had joined two years earlier. He soon became an adviser and secretary to Bonifacio on account of his brilliant mind and forceful character. Women had been admitted and included, among others, the wife of Bonifacio and two sisters of Rizal. In the meantime Rizal, in Dapitan, had kept himself aloof from political activity and settled down to other interests, but still desired his freedom and the withdrawal of the charge of disloyalty to Spain. In 1895 he offered his services as a doctor to the Spanish army in Cuba but did not receive an immediate reply. At the beginning of 1896 the Katipunan published its revolutionary newspaper, *Kalayaan*, with contributions from Bonifacio, Jacinto and Pio Valenzuela. A few months later Valenzuela, who was a physician, was sent to Dapitan to obtain Rizal's support. The official reason for the visit was professional consultation. Rizal, according to reports, did not approve of active rebellion. Shortly after meeting Valenzuela, Rizal received a letter from the governor-general, Ramon Blanco, notifying him that the Spanish authorities had accepted his offer to serve in Cuba. Leaving almost immediately, Rizal arrived in Manila on 6 August, but was ordered to remain aboard a Spanish warship.

Valenzuela's report that Rizal was against rebellion was received with consternation. About a week after Rizal's arrival in Manila denunciations concerning the existence of the Katipunan reached the authorities and resulted in the discovery of the office of the society. Though suspects were rounded up, Bonifacio, Jacinto and others were able to go into hiding. At a party meeting Bonifacio urged open resistance.[23] Messages were sent to different parts of the country and four days later a force led by Bonifacio attacked a Spanish garrison just outside Manila. The Philippine Revolution had begun. The same day Blanco, proclaimed a state of war in the provinces of Manila, Bulacan, Pampanga, Nueva Ecija, Tarlac, Laguna, Batangas and Cavite, where the revolutionaries, under their local leader, Emilio Aguinaldo, achieved success to a degree unrivalled in any other province.

Unfortunately this success soon led to rivalry and the splitting of the Katipunan into two factions. As a revolutionary, Bonifacio was a determined and tireless Filipino who pursued the goal of freedom for his country. As a military and political leader he was unsuccessful and unable to check the reverses and political intrigue within the Katipunan. This lost him not only the leadership of the movement to Aguinaldo but eventually his life at the hands of his own associates.

46

He was executed by armed followers of Aguinaldo on 10 May 1897, following charges of sedition.

Rizal, who was still in Manila awaiting permission to leave for Cuba when the revolt broke out, disassociated himself from the uprising and was allowed to leave Manila for Spain on 3 September. His loyalty to Spain was soon questioned, following the interrogation of Katipunan prisoners. On arrival in Spain, Rizal was immediately arrested and sent back to Manila for trial on charges of illicit associations and the stirring up of rebellion against the Spanish government. On 26 December 1896 he appeared before a military court, was declared guilty as charged and condemned to death. The Spanish authorities, by carrying out the sentence, virtually ensured their own doom by making Rizal a martyr and a national hero.

The Spanish failed to halt the revolutionaries who, led by Aguinaldo, continued the struggle against superior military forces. The more the Filipinos suffered reverses the harder they resisted. The new governor-general, Primo de Rivera, realized that military strength alone could not crush the rebellion. Following the establishment of a Republic at Biak-na-Bato in Bulacan province on 1 November 1897, he initiated peace negotiations with leading Filipinos. Aguinaldo, knowing that the future of the movement was uncertain agreed to a truce and the pact of Biak-na-Bato was signed on 14 and 15 December, the revolutionary leaders agreeing to go into exile in Hong Kong in return for a general amnesty. In addition, a monetary indemnity was to be paid to the nationalists and compensation given to civilian families who had suffered as a result of the conflict. Finally, a promise was exacted that Spain would introduce municipal reforms and grant individual rights.

4   American intervention

In EARLY 1898, when Aguinaldo and his followers had gone to Hong Kong, peace in the Philippines proved to be illusory. Contrary to the amnesty, many of the Filipinos who had surrendered their arms were arrested and persecuted. Sporadic revolts once more began to break out to fan a widespread nationalist feeling which culminated in acts of sabotage. About this time events in Cuba and the American support of the Cuban revolutionary movement led by José Marti, foreshadowed United States intervention in the Philippines. A small group led by the American under-secretary of the navy, Theodore Roosevelt, Senator Henry Cabot Lodge and the naval historian Alfred Mahan was convinced that the Spanish empire was disintegrating and saw an opportunity to secure an American base in Southeast Asia. Alfred Ravenholt writes, 'before proceeding to take command of the U.S. Asiatic squadron, Commodore Dewey had made an intensive study of the charts of Philippine waters and his naval vessels were in a high state of readiness for the opportunity afforded by hostilities'.[24] Aguinaldo was already aware of American intentions and made an agreement with Dewey for American assistance against the Spanish.

On 15 February 1898, in circumstances never clearly established, the United States cruiser *Maine* blew up in the Cuban port of Havana. Because of the growing belief that it was the manifest destiny of the United States to supervise the welfare of Cuba, Congress passed resolutions declaring Cuba to be independent, and not only demanded the withdrawal of Spain but directed the President to use the army and navy if he deemed it necessary. On 20 April, President McKinley approved an ultimatum demanding

48

Spanish withdrawal from Cuba and a reply before noon of 23 April. War was declared by the Spanish government on 24 April. Next day the United States Congress announced that hostilities had existed since 21 April. The American squadron waiting near Hong Kong sailed for the Philippines and entered Manila Bay on 1 May. In the ensuing naval battle the Spanish fleet, commanded by Admiral Patricio Montojo, was destroyed and the Americans took possession of Cavite pending the arrival of a land force to capture Manila.

Richard Hofstadter has written, 'it was at Roosevelt's insistence and without authorization from his superior, Secretary of State J. D. Long, that Admiral Dewey launched his attack upon the Spanish fleet in the Philippines'.[25] The Spanish governor-general, Basilio Augustin, made frantic appeals to the Filipinos for their support, but in vain. Aguinaldo now urged the people to rise against the Spanish and support the Americans in the belief that they had come as liberators. With the assistance of Dewey, Aguinaldo and the other exiles returned to the Philippines on 19 May and within a few weeks Aguinaldo was again at the head of Filipino forces. The Filipino militia, which had been organized by the Spaniards, deserted, and their defeat and demoralization soon enabled the revolutionaries to capture the greater part of Luzon, with Manila the main objective.

On 12 June a proclamation of Philippine Independence was made at Kawit, in Cavite, and the Philippine flag unfurled for the first time to the accompanying strains of the new national anthem. Unfortunately for the Filipinos the United States had been given the opportunity to secure a foothold in the Far East at a time of worldwide expansionist competition between the European powers and the United States to secure territory. Senator William Fulbright has written, 'The United States went to war in 1898 for the stated purpose of liberating Cuba from Spanish tyranny, but after winning the war . . . the United States brought the liberated Cubans under an American protectorate and incidentally annexed the Philippines because, according to President McKinley, the Lord told him it was America's duty "to educate the Filipinos, and uplift and civilize and Christianize them" . . .'.[26]

Following the arrival of American troops to augment the Filipino forces besieging Manila, the fate of the city was sealed. On 13 August 1898, the Spanish defenders surrendered and the American forces entered the city. The Filipinos were kept outside by order of the American and Spanish commissioners, who negotiated the terms of surrender, and later that day the American flag was hoisted and the Spanish flag hauled down. This action by the Americans caused bitter disillusionment among the Filipinos. Peace discussions between the Americans and the Spaniards ended in the signing of the Treaty of Paris in December 1898. Though Aguinaldo had sent a Filipino lawyer, Felipe Agoncillo, to Paris to plead the case for independence, he was not allowed to attend the peace conference. With the signing of the treaty, Spain renounced unconditionally all sovereign rights over Cuba and Puerto Rico and ceded the Philippines to the United States for a $20 million indemnity.*

Hoping that the United States Senate would not ratify the treaty, Aguinaldo sent Agoncillo to Washington to canvass support for their independence. Meanwhile the Filipinos were determined to show the Americans that they meant business, and on 23 January 1899 they established the First Philippine Republic at Malolos which, although unrecognized by the United States, soon claimed substantial jurisdiction throughout the archipelago, particularly in Luzon. Its constitution included a bill of rights, with executive power being vested in a president assisted by seven ministers and legislative power, in a representative assembly.

Relations between the Filipinos and the Americans grew steadily worse and, on the night of 4 February 1899, a Filipino soldier was killed by an American soldier for a reason not clear, causing the inevitable conflict between the two forces to break out. In the United States, news of the outbreak created an anti-Filipino

* Amounts of money will be expressed throughout in U.S. dollars. The rate of exchange in 1898 was $4.85 to the pound sterling. On writing the rate of exchange is $2.40 to the pound. The current rate of exchange for the Philippine peso is 3 pesos 93 centavos to the dollar and 90 pesos 60 centavos to the pound.

50

hysteria and influenced the Senate to ratify the Treaty of Paris and support the government in its decision to pacify the Philippines by military means.

Bombarded by the American fleet and facing superior forces, the Filipinos were forced to leave Manila in disorder. American troops under General A. MacArthur took to the offensive and captured Malolos on 31 March 1899, but Aguinaldo had already moved the seat of government to San Fernando, Pampanga. In their fight against the Americans the Filipinos were under the command of Antonio Luna, who had earlier studied military tactics and strategy in Europe. Unfortunately he was hampered in his efforts because of the jealousy and distrust of Aguinaldo, and he eventually suffered the same fate as Bonifacio, being murdered by associates of Aguinaldo. After Luna's death, Aguinaldo took command of the military operations, but disaster now followed disaster and it became necessary for the Filipinos to break up into small guerrilla bands. This forced the Americans to continue the struggle until, by a ruse, they were able to capture Aguinaldo in March 1901. By the middle of 1902 the majority of the revolutionaries had given up their cause as lost.

Despite some concern in Congress the United States President, William McKinley, had decided that the Philippines should remain in American hands and sent a commission led by Jacob G. Schurman, President of Cornell University, to survey conditions in the islands in 1899. Owing to the unsettled military position, very little was achieved. Towards the middle of 1900 another commission was sent, with Judge William H. Taft as Chairman. During this time a number of prominent Filipinos formed a political party, called the Federal Party, to work for collaboration with the Americans. Among them was Pedro A. Paterno, who had also been instrumental in negotiating the pact between Aguinaldo and Primo de Rivera in 1897. Many of the leaders of the revolution refused to associate with the Federal Party or collaborate with the Americans, and to check possible opposition to peace moves MacArthur had many of them deported to Guam. The most notable was Apolinario Mabini, who had been Aguinaldo's chief adviser since 1898. The pattern of

51

American rule in the archipelago was set by William Taft as President of the Philippine Commission during the years 1901–04, with a policy similar to MacArthur's and leading towards complete independence, a policy Taft followed as War Secretary under President Theodore Roosevelt. As President of the Commission, Taft faced immense difficulties in the country which was suffering from the aftermath of long and bloody struggles, the spread of epidemics, drought and food shortages. Though the capture of Aguinaldo had dealt a severe blow to the revolutionaries, scattered revolts and banditry continued. Trade declined and the silver Mexican currency used during the Spanish era had lost its value. The Philippine Commission continued the measures initiated by General A. Mac-Arthur, to prepare the ground for a free and independent Republic and a free primary school system. Plans were made for the expansion of government health services. Steps were taken to stage local elections as a means of consulting Filipino opinion and ensuring their participation in local government. Taft worked hard to ensure the passage through Congress in 1902 of the Philippine Bill, or Cooper Act, which extended the Bill of Rights to the Filipinos, though trial by jury and the right to bear arms were omitted. Immediately afterwards President Roosevelt proclaimed the end of the war and preparations were made for a census prior to the establishment of a Legislative Assembly. A large number of American teachers arrived and English was introduced in Philippine classrooms.

In 1903 the United States agreed to a relief fund of $3 million and the Philippines Currency Act was passed linking the peso to the gold standard. Taft was succeeded in 1904 by Luke E. Wright, who became the first American to bear the title of governor-general in Manila. More and more Filipinos gave their support to the work of the American commission, and a number were appointed members. Many of the American administrators tried hard to create a Philippine Civil Service. Nevertheless, the spirit of nationalism was very much alive and growing in expression. The paternalistic policy of the United States was no substitute for the coveted independence. A number of political parties had emerged after the proclamation of peace in 1902 to keep alive the sentiment

52

of a majority of the People and to counteract the pro-American Federal Party.

In the Sulu Archipelago the Americans had not succeeded any better than the Spanish in pacifying the Muslims with their policy of military persuasion and force. Further difficulties were encountered with the Roman Catholic church over the question of land ownership and the United States' declared policy of separation of church and state. Agrarian unrest had increased once more when many of the friars began to reoccupy former holdings, despite Taft's proposal that such lands should be purchased by the government and sold in small lots to occupying tenants. Finally, after lengthy negotiations with the papal authorities, agreement was reached towards the end of 1903 for the purchase of a major portion of the lands for more than $7 million, the money being raised by the issue of bonds. The Spanish archbishop and bishops were also replaced by American prelates.

The determined American effort to develop free and secular education followed the pattern of that in the United States and fulfilled a Filipino demand that had for a long time been unsatisfied. Non-Christian Filipinos were given equal opportunities and the Catholic schools and colleges established by the Spanish were allowed to continue. In 1903 the Bureau of Education was set up to organize the educational system and encourage Filipinos to learn the English language. Many of the Spanish-speaking *élite* quickly adapted themselves to the new administration and became outwardly pro-American. In the provincial towns and rural areas, however, the people with their deeply rooted native way of thinking and speaking their own dialect in the home, showed little interest in learning English or Spanish. They distrusted central government and ideas aimed at modernization. Their social, economic and religious activities were centred on the home. Knowledge and wisdom within the family was equated with age. Nevertheless, slight progress was made and the teacher became a respected member of the community.

In 1906 the ban against political parties advocating independence was lifted. In anticipation of elections for the first Assembly, two nationalist parties united to form a single party, *Partido Nacionalista*, in opposition to the pro-American *Partido Nacional Progresista*, formerly known as the Federal Party. The game of politics introduced by the Americans had taken firm hold among the Filipinos. In the elections the Partido Nacionalista won 59 seats against 16 for the Progresistas and 5 for the Independents. There was great excitement when Taft arrived in Manila to inaugurate the first Philippine Assembly in the Opera House on 16 October 1907. At the inauguration Taft committed the United States to a policy that would eventually give the Filipinos control over public affairs and lead to independence with equal rights for rich and poor alike. He expressed the hope that the Americans would be able to stay long enough to finish the task of educating the people and training them for the tasks of responsible administration.

The founder of the winning Nacionalista Party, Sergio Osmeña, was elected Speaker of the Assembly, a post that he was to hold for fifteen years. His close friend, Manuel L. Quezon, was chosen as the majority floor leader. The Philippine Assembly was granted from the beginning a considerable influence in deciding issues concerning, judicial administration and domestic legislation. The first bill passed was the Gabaldon Law, which appropriated a million pesos for the development of *barrio* (village) schools. In accordance with provisions in the Cooper Act, the Philippines could now be represented in the United States Congress by two commissioners without voting rights. The first two Filipinos to be appointed were Benito Legarda and Pablo Ocampo.

Achievements in trade, compared to political progress, were less satisfactory. By 1910 a mercantilism had emerged which favoured American goods and shipping, and levied taxes on the export of basic Philippine goods. This applied as well to import duties on products competing with those of United States origin. There were protests from the commissioners, but nothing was done to change the American monopoly of trade. Large investments were made in developing sugar, tobacco, timber, oils and abaca. The Americans relied on the free play of economic forces and made no serious attempt to change the old-established pattern of land ownership.

54

Thus the caciques were able to maintain a strong position in the new political and economic life of the Philippine archipelago.

In 1912, when Woodrow Wilson became the U.S. President, he appointed Francis Burton Harrison, as the new governor of the Philippines, to carry out a policy of liberalization and accelerate the process of independence by giving the Filipinos more responsibilities. Filipinos who supported the Nationalist Party leaders were given five out of nine seats in the Philippine Commission, which became in reality a quasi-administrative upper house. Harrison also adopted a civil service policy of replacing Americans with Filipinos. In 1916 the United States Congress passed the Jones Act. For the Filipinos this meant an enlargement of the popular franchise and an elective Senate to serve as the upper house of the legislature in place of the commission. Executive power of government was, however, vested in the governor. The Philippine legislature now consisted of a Senate with 24 members and a House of Representatives with 92 members. The Jones Act stated that the Filipinos would be given their independence as soon as they had demonstrated that they could govern themselves.

Francis Harrison was completely free of racial prejudice and cultivated Filipino friendship. However, his conviction that more Filipinos should avail themselves of opportunities to participate in government was unrealistic. Because of the social domination of the caciques only a few Filipinos could take advantage of his policy. Many of these were intellectuals, with a following, who quickly discovered that a parliamentary constitution was not only a platform to express their political views but a convenient means of maintaining their position and vanity. By 1920, when the civil service had been almost 'filipinized', it was found that many employees were related and that government positions were being bought or secured through political influence. Corruption became widespread and has continued with few exceptions to the present day. Onofre D. Corpuz has written, 'The historical roots—graft and corruption—derived directly from the character of the relationship between the government and Filipino society during the Spanish colonial experience ... many offices of government were sold. ... The post of secretary to the municipal board of Manila sold for 12,000 pesos in 1632 and for almost 14,000 pesos in 1730 . . . The morality arising from such a system is easily imagined'.[27]

In the United States a Republican, Warren G. Harding, had succeeded Wilson as president. President Harding, who was a protégé of commercial interests and conservatism, benefited from the feeling of weariness in the United States at the end of the First World War. There had been a strong reaction against the idealism of Wilson, and consequently the conduct of affairs in the Philippines under Harrison was critically reviewed by the new administration. An investigating mission was sent to the islands, which reported political and governmental instability and the need to postpone independence. Towards the end of 1921 General Leonard Wood replaced Harrison as governor-general and soon antagonized the members of the legislature by exercising his right to veto legislation. The Filipinos were in no mood to turn the clock back to the pre-Harrison era and have their responsibilities curtailed. Growing tension precipitated an open break late in 1923 when the Senate president, Manuel Quezon, the Speaker, Sergio Osmeña, and the other Filipino officials resigned from the Council of State. Wood allowed their resignations to stand, entrusted routine work to under-secretaries and abolished the council. He administered the country through a group of his own, drawn mostly from military personnel, firmly supported by Washington. Differences developed on economic matters and, openly affirming his opposition to government control over business, Wood annulled the Board of Control, set up earlier, by Harrison, to supervise the state-owned corporations. This involved the Manila Railway, National Bank and cement factories as well as coal-mines and sugar distribution centres. After the board's abolition, Wood alone, controlled the government stocks. Though he had little regard for the Filipinos, Wood was an efficient administrator, and not only checked corruption in the government but carried through a large programme of public works with emphasis on education and the improvement of health facilities.

Opposing political parties, the Nacionalista and Democrata, now united in a common fight against the governor and pressed the

United States Congress to interfere, but without result. The dead-lock was in the end resolved by the death of Wood in 1927. The next governor-general was Henry L. Stimson, who was able to restore co-operation with the local leaders during his one year of office. He revived the Council of State and increased its membership to include the majority floor leaders of the two Houses. Stimson was succeeded by Dwight F. Davis; and in 1932 Theodore Roosevelt Jr. became governor-general and carried on Stimson's more liberal policies.

External trade and commerce had expanded during two decades mainly as a result of American domination of the economy. The import business was largely in their hands, although Chinese, British and other nationalities had their share. Despite the decision of the United States to extend to the Philippines its own immigration laws and thus restrict the flow of Chinese immigrants, many American business concerns were anxious to secure Chinese labour. Although the Chinese were regarded as aliens and the object of widespread fear and jealousy, their skill as traders and money-lenders was apparent. They had control over the greater part of the retail trade and owned a large proportion of the rice mills.

Less conspicuous was the increasing number of Japanese settlers in the Mountain Province, mostly market gardeners, and in the Davao district of Mindanao. Here they steadily extended and improved the cultivation of abaca and the developing of lumbering and deep-sea fishing. Filipino workers, however, had little share in the economic prosperity and lived in a state of poverty and ignorance which precipitated recurring unrest. The Americans, while promoting communications and basic utilities, still believed in unfettered private enterprise and the free play of economic forces. They did nothing to change the established pattern of land-holding.

The collapse of the New York stock market in 1929, and the possible curtailment of the free market of the United States, brought home to the Filipino leaders the danger to the Philippine economy and the pressing need for economic security. Already American farm interests and producers of other products were pressing for safeguards against free trade. They favoured the granting of Philippine independence as a move to close the door to duty-free imports from the archipelago. The American labour unions also supported Philippine independence, motivated by a wish to stop Filipino emigrants competing with American labour. Extensive lobbying by these interests resulted in a Philippine independence bill, called the Hare-Hawes-Cutting Act, being passed by both Houses of Congress. Though vetoed by President Hoover, it was passed again over the veto in January 1933 and was finally submitted to the Philippine legislature for approval. Disagreement now arose between the Filipino leaders Osmeña, Roxas and Aquino, who had supported the bill in Washington, and Manuel Quezon, who opposed it because of the provision granting military and naval bases in the archipelago. In 1933 President Franklin D. Roosevelt appointed Frank Murphy as governor-general, who was known as a strong advocate of Philippine independence. Quezon still opposed the bill over the question of bases, and in October the Philippine legislature rejected it. A month later Quezon led a mission to Washington to negotiate a new bill with the Roosevelt administration.

After some months of frustrating discussion, a compromise bill was submitted. This omitted the provision for naval bases but was more or less a duplicate of its predecessor. Known as the Tydings-McDuffie Act, it was passed by both Houses of Congress, received presidential approval on 24 March 1934 and was ratified some two months later by the Philippine legislature. The bill established a Philippine Commonwealth, provided for independence after a transition period of ten years, a graduated tax on Philippine exports to the United States and a bill of rights, and authorized a constitutional convention for the Philippines. This decision to grant early independence was one of the first steps taken by President Roosevelt to satisfy domestic criticism of free trade and to appease anti-colonial feeling. The provision that the question of bases would be the subject of later negotiations was seen in Manila as a personal victory for Quezon.

Frank Murphy, proclaimed 10 July 1934 as the day for the election of delegates to the constitutional convention, and on 30 July the convention was formally opened. The constitution was signed on 19 February 1935 and was ratified by popular vote in the Philippines on

14 May the same year. The governor-general, Frank Murphy, now became the first American high commissioner and could intervene if necessary and protect American interests. At the same time he was obliged to vacate and hand over his official residence, Malacañang, to the Commonwealth president and leave political initiative to the Filipinos.[28] The constitution, as drafted, was on the whole a praiseworthy document, although certain aspects concerning suffrage could be questioned. It was based on the fundamental principles of social justice, rights for the people and the separation of the legislative, executive and judicial powers.

Manuel Quezon had now become the dominant figure in politics and was elected as the first President with Sergio Osmeña as Vice-President. Quezon's ideals of liberty and social justice captured the people's imagination, and the majority of working people saw at last a chance to obtain better economic security, a release from penury and privation. For those who have less in life to have more in law, that was their hope when the inauguration of the Commonwealth took place in November 1935. It was an important date in the turbulent history of the archipelago.

The economic provisions of the Tydings-McDuffie Act and the American retention of control, through the high commissioner, over finance, customs and defence, soon cast a dark shadow over the optimistic thoughts of full independence in ten years. It became obvious that to avoid economic disaster Philippine exports would have to continue to receive preferential tariffs. In 1936 Frank Murphy was succeeded as high commissioner by Paul V. McNutt, who was convinced that it was a mistake to grant the Philippines full independence. He tried hard to change the official policy but without success. In 1937, a Joint Preparatory Committee on Philippine Affairs was set up to study the economic problems involved and make recommendations. The result was new legislation by Congress in 1939 to amend provisions of the Tydings-McDuffie Act and to extend preferential trade relations.

After the inauguration of Quezon as President, active steps were taken by the Commonwealth government to reorganize the executive. New councils were established for economic relief, education, defence as well as an institute of national language and a commission for Mindanao and Salu. A law was passed providing for compulsory military service and the organization of the Philippine armed forces. General Douglas MacArthur, son of General Arthur MacArthur, was appointed military adviser to the Commonwealth government and made a field-marshal in the Philippine army. Though he had served as commander of the Philippine department during the years 1928-30 and as chief of staff at Washington, he did not appear to have taken seriously the Japanese threat to Asia, despite the tension caused by an unprovoked attack in 1937 on the United States gunboat *Panay* in the river above Nanking, and the Japanese Mobilization Act of 1938.

President Quezon showed from the beginning concern for social justice. Revenues from United States refunds of excise and processing taxes on sugar and oils were used for a large programme of public works and the purchase of land for settlement. Laws were enacted which granted more rights to the working class and the provision of legal assistance for the poor. Energetic efforts were made to promote agriculture and mining, the production of cigars, lumber, copra, oils and fats. Producers were aided in the marketing and distribution of their products. In 1940 Sulu became a part of the Commonwealth following the signing of a treaty abolishing the sultanate. About the same time amendments to the constitution were proposed by the Nacionalista Party, approved by the legislature and by popular vote. Two features of the original constitution were amended by provisions for a four-year term of office for both the president and vice-president and for the establishment of a bicameral Congress with the Senate elected by national vote and the House of Representatives elected by district voting. An Independent Commission on Elections was also established. Following President Roosevelt's approval, Quezon proclaimed the changes to the constitution.

Following the outbreak of war in Europe in 1939, the Japanese invasion of French Indo-China a year later and Japan's signing of the triple alliance with Germany and Italy, the United States reacted by freezing Japanese assets and declaring an embargo on oil. With tension mounting in the Pacific, MacArthur was recalled to active duty to command the United States and Philippine forces. Japanese ambitions in Asia became clearer with the appointment of General Hideki Tojo as Prime Minister and virtual dictator. Unaware of the imminent danger, the Filipinos were caught up in the throes of the first elections to be held under the amended constitution. As expected, the Nacionalista Party was again victorious and Quezon and Osmeña were re-elected in November 1941 for a four-year term.

On 8 December news was received of the surprise attack on Pearl Harbor. Almost simultaneously with the news Japanese air squadrons began to bomb various points in the islands including Davao, Baguio, Tarlac and the major airbase at Clark Field, north of Manila. Within two days Japanese aircraft had destroyed the greater part of the American air strength and reduced the naval base at Cavite to a heap of smouldering ruins. On 21 December the main invasion force landed in northern Luzon. Every effort was made to delay the Japanese advance towards Manila, but without air support the Filipino and American troops were forced to retire to Bataan and Corregidor. Disaster was almost complete as the outcome on Bataan was inevitable. It is reported that President Quezon considered an appeal to declare the Philippines neutral but was persuaded to allow himself to be evacuated to the United States.

Following the entry of the Japanese and the declaration of Manila as an open city in January 1942, Quezon, accompanied by Osmeña and other members of the cabinet, left Corregidor by submarine on the night of 20 February on the first stage of the long journey to Washington. A month later MacArthur was ordered by Roosevelt to leave for Australia, and General Jonathan Wainwright became commander of all forces left in the islands. For nearly five months Filipino and American troops, outnumbered and lacking ammunition, food and medical supplies, fought a magnificent defensive action against far superior forces. On 9 April 1942 Bataan fell and a month later Corregidor was overrun. This marked the end of organized resistance against the Japanese. After his surrender, Wainwright was sent as a prisoner of war to Formosa. Many troops, however, refused to obey his surrender order and hid in the jungles and mountains of the archipelago interior, where they formed guerrilla bands. Supported by a majority of the people, despite privation and acute shortages of equipment, they harassed the Japanese forces and carried out widespread sabotage. By the end of 1942 some of the guerrillas were able to make radio contact with the Allied forces concentrated in Australia under MacArthur's command.

From the start the Japanese expected to be welcomed as liberators and were eager to win to their side as many of the Filipinos as possible by courting political and religious spokesmen. The emphasis was on Asia for the Asiatics. Every effort was made to gain Filipino collaboration in a policy of eradicating the age-old notion of Western supremacy. Japanese long-term policies were, however, contradicted by their military colonialism that was more ruthless than the American rule had been. Exactions of food supplies bore heavily on the Filipinos, whose economic condition was rapidly deteriorating as a result of the circulation of paper money and spiralling inflation. Agrarian unrest, already a problem in the Philippines, was given added impetus. Many of the tenant farmers and workers saw a chance to redress by concerted action the abuse by moneylenders and cacique landlords who had for long dominated agriculture and politics. Thus was born the Hukong Bayan Laban Sa Hapon (Huk) guerrilla movement under the leadership of Luis Taruc in central Luzon. Popularly known as the Anti-Japanese Army or Hukbalahap, it was partly communist led but drew most of its support from the impoverished tenant farmers.

Following the occupation of Manila, the Japanese High Command, led by General Homma, ordered the mayor, Jorge Vargas, to organize a civil government.[29] In January 1942 the Philippine Executive Commission was established, consisting of Vargas, Benigno Aquino, Alas, Rafael Alunan, José Laurel, Claro Recto, Quintin Paredes and José Yulo. In accordance with a promise given by the Japanese prime minister during a visit to Manila in 1943, a Preparatory Commission for Philippine Independence (PCPI) was formed to draft a constitution for independence.[30] The constitution was, with the exception of new clauses to suit the Japanese, similar to the original 1935 constitution and provided an article which stipulated that another constitution would be drafted within one year of the

62

ending of hostilities. In September 1943 the National Assembly met and elected José Laurel as President of the Republic of the Philippines, inaugurated on 14 October. The Philippine flag was now raised for the first time during the Japanese occupation. Despite intensive propaganda the new régime had little support from the majority of the people, who were bitterly anti-Japanese.

By the end of 1943 Allied strength in the Pacific had reached a point where it was possible to attack selected targets. Strategy called for an advance upon the Japanese positions from two different directions. During the first half of 1944 these two movements from different points rapidly converged, finally closing in upon the Philippines. On 20 October American forces under MacArthur landed on Leyte, in the Visayas, inflicting grievous losses, while at sea the American 3rd and 7th Fleets fought a decisive naval action. In the wake of the United States forces was Vice-President Osmeña of the pre-war Commonwealth government, who led the returning Filipinos; Quezon had died in New York nearly three months earlier. By the end of November nearly a quarter of a million troops had landed and Japanese resistance was crumbling. On 9 January a new phase of the recapture of the Philippines opened, and the Americans, reinforced by Filipino guerrillas, advanced towards Manila. For nearly three weeks in February the Japanese fought a desperate defence in which they spared neither themselves nor the civilian population in the fury of war. Manila emerged a smoking ruin and crematorium, but liberation had been achieved. Within days the Commonwealth government was restored by MacArthur. President Osmeña assumed the full powers and responsibilities in accordance with the pre-war constitution.

The Japanese were still holding out in various parts of the islands and it was not until 5 July 1945 that MacArthur could announce the liberation of the country as a whole. Fighting still continued, however, against the remnants of the Japanese Command, under General Yamashita, entrenched in the mountain fastnesses north of Baguio, and only ended with the final surrender of Japan to the Allies on 2 September 1945. During the fighting Laurel and other leaders were taken to Japan, while others found refuge with the

American forces. Following the Japanese surrender, Laurel dissolved the Japanese-sponsored republic.

President Osmeña and the Commonwealth government were faced with staggering problems of rehabilitation and reconstruction as well as social demoralization. The United States had to take measures to restore the economy. In 1946 President Truman approved the Philippine Rehabilitation (war damage) Act and a year later the Philippine Trade Act. The Rehabilitation Act included a sum of $620,000,000 to meet war claims and to finance building programmes. The Trade Act extended the period of duty-free trade until 1954, with an increase of five per cent of the full tariff rate to be applied afterwards. At the same time no change was to be made in import quotas for Philippine sugar and cordage for a period of twenty-eight years. If nothing else, the war had revealed how dependent the economy of the islands was on outside markets and assistance. American agencies were formed to extend help in restoring civil government and essential services. Shortages of food, clothing, drugs and household articles created black markets and encouraged crime. Once more the agrarian problem came into the limelight. After liberation the American military authorities treated the Hukbalahap guerrilla movement with hostility. They arrested the leader, Luis Taruc, though not for long, while finding it expedient to overlook collaboration with the Japanese on the part of a number of prominent politicians including Manuel Roxas. This blunder eventually led to bloodshed and could have been avoided if the guerrillas, who had fought with the Hukbalahap, had been properly treated and steps taken to enable them to return to a more normal life. Bitter and disillusioned, they returned to their mountain hideouts and prepared for revolutionary activity.

Immediately after the liberation Filipino politics witnessed a struggle between the rival personalities of Osmeña and Roxas. Roxas was elected President of the Commonwealth on 23 April 1946. He had the support of MacArthur, and had left the Nacionalista Party to form a new Liberal movement which took control of the administration in an atmosphere of cynicism. Notwithstanding doubts about launching the republic, the United States found it politically expedient to keep its pledge to grant full independence on 4 July. In reality, American influence would still be a dominating factor as complete economic independence would have meant bankruptcy. Despite the enormous development of trade that had taken place during the American era, the Philippines remained a typical example of Latin-American democracy where technological advances rested on a substratum of deep-rooted Spanish influence.

5   The beginning of freedom

ON THE MORNING of 4 July 1946, amidst the devastation and ruins of Manila, the new Republic of the Philippines was inaugurated. With the raising of the Philippine flag the goal of independence had at long last been achieved. The nation was free, at least in theory if not in practice. Economically dependent on the United States, the Republic was faced with the problems arising out of the chaos and destruction of war in which nearly five per cent of the population had been injured or killed. Those Filipinos remaining were weak from malnutrition and disease, with malaria and cholera taking a deadly toll. The economy was shattered and agrarian discontent and lawlessness was on the increase throughout the islands. It is not surprising that the Hukbalahap found a ready response to its plans for establishing a People's Democratic Government. Shortages of goods and the exploitation of American war-surplus material resulted in a massive black market. Many Americans and Filipinos became virtual millionaires overnight. The enormous stockpiles accumulated by the United States, in anticipation of a long war against the Japanese, were turned over to the Philippine government for a nominal sum; the government in turn quickly capitalized on the opportunity to finance party expenses and bolster individual wealth and influence. The example of congressmen and senators, who were openly involved in deals helped the Hukbalahap by their scandals, and at the same time encouraged the abuses which are still evident in the archipelago today. The desire for wealth became increasingly important to those in official positions.

Manuel Roxas, who had the support of the Americans and the majority of the wealthy landowners, was, like earlier politicians, reluctant to introduce serious agrarian reform. A sop, however, was

66

offered towards the end of 1946 with the passing of the Tenancy Act which ostensibly provided that the tenant was to receive 70 per cent and the landowner 30 per cent of the value of crops. Ambiguities in the act favoured the landowner and enforcement was almost impossible. Loss of confidence in the government increased when the Roxas' administration prevented a number of congressmen, elected with Hukbalahap support in Luzon, from taking their seats, accusing them of terrorism and fraud in the elections. Not surprisingly one of those unseated was Luis Taruc, the leader of the Hukbalahap. This move by Roxas was made to ensure the smooth passage of the Parity Amendment to the constitution, which among other things accorded equal rights to American citizens until 1974. This proposal had met with strong criticism from a number of Filipinos. In fact, Roxas narrowly escaped assassination on 10 March 1947, when a hand-grenade was thrown during a speech in support of the proposed amendment.

With American assistance, plans were made for the economic rehabilitation of the islands and the establishment of a central bank which could be used for monetary control. The main problem of agrarian unrest and the poverty of the great mass of people was dealt with by ordering the army and police to seek out and destroy the Hukbalahap. No distinction was made between the communist and the tenant with a genuine grievance.

Filipino against Filipino was a tragic feature of the first years of independence and pin-pointed the failure of the government and its subservience to the caciques. The Hukbalahap had now an estimated following of 150,000 centred in the four Luzon provinces of Bulacan, Nueva Ecija, Pampanga and Tarlac. They were well armed, and though some of the leaders were avowed communists the majority were former guerrillas and impoverished workers.

President Roxas died in 1948 from a heart attack and was succeeded by the vice-president, Elpidio Quirino, a veteran politician loyal to his party. This meant a continuation of the policy of inaction in solving the problems of the Hukbalahap and land tenure, as well as tacit approval of graft carried on by various members of the government and their friends. Although subject to the dictates of his party,

67

Quirino was, nevertheless, well intentioned. Born of humble parents, he was not a member of the caciques. His attempt to negotiate a settlement with the Hukbalahap, with an offer of amnesty, failed because of the deep suspicion already engendered on both sides and the changing demands of the Hukbalahap leaders, who were becoming more and more confident of success in their struggle. The government had little support from the people, largely because of the lack of discipline in the army units, who in their eager search for rebels repeatedly abused and antagonized the rural population. Many landowners formed their own security forces to do their bidding under the cloak of self-defence and protection, usually with the connivance and help of local police commanders.

Quirino completed the remainder of Roxas's term of office as president, and with Liberal support successfully contested the presidential election in November 1949 by defeating the Nacionalist candidate, José P. Laurel. It was a campaign characterized by false electoral returns, flagrant intimidation of voters and the use of armed gangs to beat or kill the supporters of the opposition. These tactics besmirched the good name of the Philippines and aroused outside indignation. The campaign was described by a former American judge of the Supreme Court of the Philippines as the 'dirtiest and bloodiest in Philippine election campaigns'.[31] Rash promises had been made by candidates concerning rural reconstruction, fully aware as they were that the administration was bankrupt. With a national treasury that was empty, and the wages of government employees months in arrears, official corruption increased during 1950 to unprecedented heights, helped by the stopping of programmes of public works, falling copra prices and the urgent need for government control to save the dwindling reserves of foreign exchange. While many businessmen made enormous fortunes, the great mass of Filipinos continued to live in abject poverty and disillusionment—ideal conditions for breeding agitation, disorder and a belief in communism. The example of China and the outbreak of the Korean civil war during the summer of 1950 had given the necessary impetus to the Hukbalahap. Taruc

68

now decided that the time was opportune and changed the name of the movement to Hukbong Mapagpalaya ng Bayan or People's Army of Liberation, referred to as the Huks.

From secret headquarters in Manila, plans were formulated for the overthrow of the Quirino régime, with its American advisers, and for the establishment of a popular government. Among the leaders of the movement were the Lava brothers, one of whom, Vincente an active guerrilla during the Japanese occupation, was an ardent admirer of the methods used by Mao Tse-tung and the Chinese communists. Attacks widened in scope. In parts of Luzon the Huks more or less carried on a form of local government, levying taxes and obtaining financial or other support, sometimes with and sometimes without extortion from the community or from Chinese traders. Extra income was obtained by raiding and plundering selected estates, small towns and barrios controlled by large landowners.

Towards the end of 1950, lack of faith in the government was widespread and was not improved by the decision to involve the Philippines in the Korean conflict and the signing of the Quirino-Foster agreement with the United States. This agreement not only provided financial and technical aid for rehabilitation but permitted the stationing of American advisers in virtually all branches of government, including the establishment of a Joint Military Advisory Group. To the outsider this was not a surprise. United States Far East policy since the end of the Second World War had been to retain its position as the major Western power in the area as a bulwark against Chinese communism. Recognition had already been given to Vietnam, Cambodia and Laos, and steps taken to undermine French influence by sending another military advisory group to Saigon after the beginning of the Korean war. In the Philippines the Huks were a threat to American air, naval and military bases as well as commercial interests. To suppress the Huk revolt meant a complete reorganization of the Philippine army and the provision of sufficient funds to maintain its effectiveness. An American loan was arranged, and Quirino was advised to appoint a former guerrilla leader and congressman, Ramon Magsaysay, the son of a Zambales artisan, as Secretary of National Defence. With the assistance of other former guerrillas, Magsaysay quickly reorganized the army. Convinced that the majority of the rebel Huks were not politically minded communists, he showed remarkable foresight in a programme designed to bring the rebellion to an end while taking measures to regain their confidence by a promise of reform and resettlement. A large number reacted favourably and surrendered. Those who could show that they had not committed specified crimes were assisted in obtaining land and financial help to put it to good use. Within a few months many of the Huk leaders, including José Lava, had been caught, although it was not until 1954 that Taruc surrendered. During 1951 the Huk rebellion spread to a number of regions beyond central Luzon and included Leyte, Mindanao, Mindoro, Negros and Panay, but it gradually petered out as a result of Magsaysay's tactics. By the end of the year the backbone of the revolt had been broken and the Huks, split into separate bands, retired to the hills and mountain hideouts.

Magsaysay had shown himself to be a dynamic leader. His identification with the common people and understanding of their grievances slowly restored public confidence in the government through his example. Supported by the Americans, in particular, Colonel Edward Lansdale, he persuaded the Quirino administration to adopt serious welfare programmes for the poverty-stricken barrios and to use the armed forces in reconstruction and rehabilitation projects for the rural areas. Magsaysay's personality had swept through the country like a breath of fresh air and he found ready support from many organisations, as well as the radio, in exposing the evils of corruption and the need to clean up the government. With the approach of the 1951 senatorial elections, a National Movement for Free Elections was formed with the approval of President Quirino, and the active support of Magsaysay, to ensure that the violence and scandals of the 1949 elections would not be repeated. The result was startling. The use of the army and the police resulted not only in a free and peaceful election but in a landslide victory for the opposition Nacionalista Party which gained control of the Senate from the Liberals.

70

Ramon Magsaysay emerged as the man of the people, with a genuine desire for reform, a policy which relied on 'all-out force and an offer of friendship in dealing with the Huks'. This policy also gave impetus to many of the new professional middle-class not connected with the conservative attitudes of the traditional élite of landowners. Magsaysay's successful handling of the Huks, his concern for reform and justice for the common man revealed in him a potential president. However, he was fully aware that despite his achievements the Liberals would never allow him to go too far in accomplishing his ambition to solve the land-tenure problem and at the same time become president. At a secret conference in November 1952, held by party leaders, among whom were Senator José Laurel and Senator Claro M. Recto, Magsaysay accepted an invitation to change sides and stand as the Nacionalista candidate for the presidency. While the Nacionalista move was partly motivated as a gesture of gratitude for Magsaysay's preservation of order during the 1951 election, it was to a great extent the result of their need to find a leader who could command national confidence. In Magsaysay they had the man who could bring them almost certain victory at the next presidential election. The Nacionalista Party, like the Liberal, was controlled by wealthy merchants and caciques; and the policy of each party differed little from that of the other. In fact, a one-party system was in force with two rival factions striving for power. While a few of the caciques had their fears about Magsaysay, the majority were confident that once he had won the election for their party they could keep him in order and prevent him from carrying out any major agrarian reforms. Magsaysay, for his part, knew that he did not have the support of the Liberals, and a change of political allegiance to the Nacionalista Party was in full accord with the traditions of political life in the Philippines, which tends to emphasize personalities rather than principles or parties. In 1953 Magsaysay resigned as secretary of defence in the Quirino administration and was almost immediately nominated by the Nationalista Party as their official presidential candidate. Magsaysay's popularity in the country was carefully exploited by his campaign planners, who initiated the Magsaysay-for-President Movement (or MPM), which

71

attracted ex-guerrillas, young professionals, students and many others who had not previously taken an interest in elections. This nation-wide organization had the indirect support of the Roman Catholic church.

Magsaysay was unremitting in his efforts to win support, his visits to the barrios and his personal approach set a precedent for future election campaigns, his concern for the common man left an indelible impression on the people and on his fellow politicians. The Nacionalista Party also received unsolicited support from the Liberals as a result of dissension within the party and the efforts of a group of influential Liberals to replace Quirino by Carlos Romulo, who had been the Philippine delegate to the United Nations and President of the General Assembly during the period 1949–50. The group decided to support Magsaysay and bargained with the Nacionalista Party to give its support to their Congressional candidates.

The result of the presidential election on 10 November 1953 was as expected. Ramon Magsaysay won with an overwhelming majority over Quirino; and his deputy, Carlos P. Garcia, likewise defeated the Liberal vice-presidential candidate, José Yulo. The Nacionalista Party had gained a large majority in an election which was notable for lack of intimidation, and violence and which was supervised with determined impartiality by a Commission of Elections. For the first time an election had aroused the interest of thousands of disillusioned Filipinos. Many, however, were unable to vote because of an anomaly in the constitution—which still exists today—restricting suffrage to those who are literate and twenty-one years old.

Magsaysay was successful in combating the growing strength of the Huks by pressing the government to grant what it had promised the people. He lost no time in introducing a number of measures to help rural reconstruction. Thousands of wells were sunk, roads improved or built. A court was set up to deal with agrarian problems and assist tenants with their legal rights. Magsaysay was determined to give the people the right to justice, and his official residence, Malacañang, was open to all who had a complaint. A

Complaints and Action Commission, under Manuel Manahan, a publisher and devoted follower of the president, was established to investigate specific cases and arrange for redress. The President had the support of the United States; loans were forthcoming to enable the rural banks and co-operative societies to help tenants free themselves from debt and reduce the evil of the moneylenders and their crippling rates of interest.

In 1954 a five-year plan introduced schemes for extending irrigation areas, giving priority to the needs of central Luzon, and for removing other weaknesses in the economy such as the excessive dependence on a number of exports, all primary products, and a retarded industrial development. Between 1954 and 1956 some 7,000 families were moved from Luzon—non-Huk—and resettled on permanent plots in Mindanao and Palawan despite local objections from the Muslim minority. A major innovation was the setting-up of a Farmers Co-operative Marketing Association—FACOMA—with a number of branches throughout the archipelago.

During 1954 a controversial bill, presented by José B. Laurel and others, was introduced to prohibit aliens or non-Filipinos from engaging in retail business, giving those already carrying on business a period of ten years to wind up their affairs. This bill, designed to change the control of the retail trade, was aimed primarily at the Chinese and was fiercely resisted by the interested parties. It was passed and became law on 19 June, thus reflecting the nationalistic sentiments of Magsaysay and the government. This measure was a surprise to many American companies and a certain amount of criticism against it was voiced in Washington. The outcome, even today, is still uncertain, as considerable pressure is being applied to bring about amendments. The furore caused by this bill was slight compared to the controversy precipitated by the introduction of land-reform bills in particular the Agricultural Tenancy Act passed in 1955 in the face of protracted opposition in the legislature. It was designed to establish a democratic agricultural economy by limiting the size of large estates, in certain cases by buying estates to resell in the form of smallholdings to tenants, thus giving greater security against illegal eviction by landowners. The act was opposed by the

73

caciques, who saw it as a threat to their economic and political power. The Tenancy Act was eventually passed, but in a mutilated form, as the landowners succeeded in introducing so many amendments that it could never have the result originally intended of helping the tenant and easing the problem of agrarian unrest. After his election as president, Magsaysay had to fight for nearly two years against the vested interests controlling the party and was continually thwarted in his efforts to carry out the reforms necessary to bring about a major change in the living standards of the masses.[32]

While at the height of his popularity Magsaysay was killed in an aircrash. A few minutes after the presidential plan had taken off from the airport of Cebu City on 17 March 1957, it crashed on a mountain. The reasons were never fully explained; there was only one survivor among the twenty-seven passengers, a reporter of a Manila newspaper, named Nestor Mata. The sudden death of Magsaysay was a great loss to the Philippines and to the band of young and enthusiastic administrators that had emerged in support of his ideas. His skilful handling of the Huks and his honest and forthright introduction of measures to meet and alleviate, where possible, the grievances of the tenant farmers and workers, had clearly shown that agrarian unrest and the appeal of communism could be countered by restoring the faith and hope of the common man in the government. President Magsaysay's constant visits to the rural areas and his recognition of the importance of the barrios brought not only thousands of new voters into the electoral system but created far-reaching precedents in the political life of the archipelago and subsequent election campaigns.

Considerable assistance had been given to Magsaysay by the Americans, and the Laurel-Langley trade agreement of 1954 gave the Filipinos the same economic rights in the United States as the Americans enjoyed in the Philippines. In foreign affairs Magsaysay had carried on the principles laid down by President Roxas, including the necessity of maintaining close relations with the United States and giving unqualified support to the American position in world politics, especially in its stand against communism. In line with American tactics in refusing to support the Geneva settlement over

Vietnam and their tacit undermining of the French position, the Philippines had taken the initiative with the United States to organize a collective defence treaty as a step to stabilize the political situation in Southeast Asia. On 8 September 1954 the representatives of eight nations had signed the Pacific Charter and the Southeast Asia Collective Defence Treaty in Manila. Signatories were Australia, France, New Zealand, Pakistan, the Philippines, Thailand, the United Kingdom and the United States. At the conclusion of the Manila Conference, President Magsaysay stated, 'through the Manila Pact and the Pacific Charter, we give assurance to our sister nations in Southeast Asia that we do not seek to defend colonialism in Asia but rather to liquidate it as speedily as possible by methods of free consent'.[33] The signing of the treaty and the birth of the Southeast Asia Treaty Organization (SEATO) meant a considerable strengthening of American military and economic influence in the area. It was the outcome of the policy laid down by the then Secretary of State, John Foster Dulles, to arrange for collective action in Asia and the containment of communism on a worldwide scale, despite the strong opposition of India and the misgivings of other members of the Colombo Plan. The Manila Treaty, according to Article VIII, defined an area covering Southeast Asia which included the entire territories of the Asian signatories and the general area of the southwest Pacific, not including, however, the Pacific area north of latitude 21° 30', which meant the exclusion of Formosa. Cambodia, Laos and Vietnam were considered areas vital to the peace and security of the signatories. To guard against the risk that a signatory might call on SEATO for aid against a non-communist aggressor, the United States appended an understanding that under the treaty it considered the term aggression as applying only to communist aggression.[34]

At about the same time the Philippines, in company with Thailand and Japan, was admitted to membership in the Colombo Plan, and a year later sent a delegation to the conference of Afro-Asian states held at Bandung, in Indonesia. The main themes of the conference were anti-Western, though misgivings about the extent of Chinese nationalism and the loyalty of the overseas Chinese were partially allayed by the conciliatory attitude adopted by the Chinese Foreign Minister, Chou En-Lai. The pro-Western stand of the Philippines and a few others in stigmatizing communism as a new form of imperialism balanced the tone and had a stabilizing influence. In 1956 the Philippine Senate ratified the San Francisco Treaty of 1951, which formally ended the war with Japan, after long and protracted negotiations over the amount of reparations. According to the Reparations Agreement, Japan promised to provide $500 million in capital equipment and a further $50 million in cash and services over a period of twenty years. Loans would be available to Filipino private enterprise from an allocation of $250 million. From the Japanese point of view the granting of loans and credits could eventually lead to economic co-operation between companies in both countries and increase the amount of Japanese commercial holdings in the archipelago.

1, 2, 3 The great variety of natural resources in the Philippines attracted the Spanish explorers and more recently has been a lure for foreign investors. This sixteenth century engraving (above) shows some of the agricultural products. Below left: an engraving of a Negrito woman—*Fille des montagnes dans l'île de Luzon*. From Spanish times the Chinese have been an important minority group throughout the islands (below right).

4 Magellan on his
voyage of discovery to
the Philippines.

5 In this allegory of the
discovery of the Philip-
pines, the Pope, Philip II
and Legazpi assume their
symbolic roles as
leaders.

6 José Rizal, whose writings inspired Philippine nationalism. His execution by the Spanish in 1896 made him a national hero.

7 Aguinaldo and fellow revolutionaries in Hong Kong after the Katipunan revolt in 1898.

8 A U.S. soldier demonstrates a rifle to Filipino patriots in the Leyte jungle. These guerrilla fighters helped to drive out the Japanese after the Second World War.

9 As defence secretary, Ramon Magsaysay checked the Hukbalahap movement and won back the resentful Huks to peaceful society by providing them with land and new opportunities. Magsaysay is on the left, talking with the American, William Pomeroy.

10, 11 In 1962 when the U.S. Congress rejected an extension of the Philippine
war-damage claim, President Macapagal shifted the Independence Day
celebrations from 4 July to 12 June. Shown here (above) with Macapagal is
Emilio Aguinaldo (93), the President of the first Philippine Republic in 1898.
Below: Carlos Garcia, President between 1957-61, at his desk. The same
nonchalant atmosphere seen here reigns in the President's office today—the
people on each side of the desk move up in progression to discuss their business.

12 Marong Church, Rizal Province, Luzon, one of the oldest churches in the archipelago.

13 Below: A new business centre, Makati, in Rizal Province.

14 Right: a Muslim mosque on Mindanao—Islamic in origin, but distinctly Filipino in ornamentation.

15 The Gate of the Chinese temple, north of Manila (far right), is one of the city's most fascinating curiosities.

16 The new National Library, Manila, built in memory of José Rizal (below right).

17 Mt. Mayon seen beyond the town of Legaspi. This is one of ten active volcanoes on the islands, which are a link in the great volcanic and coral chain of Southeast Asia.

18 Rio Hundo village in the Province of Zamboanga, Mindanao.

FOLLOWING THE untimely death of President Magsaysay, the vice-president, Carlos P. Garcia, who had also acted as secretary of foreign affairs, succeeded to the presidency. Like Magsaysay, Garcia had been active as a guerrilla leader during the Japanese occupation. A Senator of long standing, and supported by the Nacionalista Party, Garcia was an experienced politician and diplomat. On taking office he pledged himself to carry on the policies of Magsaysay. At the same time, however, he had no intention of displeasing the vested interests behind the Nacionalista Party, and carefully consolidated his position by building up his own faction within the political machine by the skilful use of presidential patronage and the release of funds for public improvements. Most of the younger followers of Magsaysay and his policies had come from the growing urban and professional groups. They now broke away from the Garcia administration and launched a new third party called the Progressive Party, nominating as their presidential candidate, Manuel Manahan.

Manahan was handicapped from the beginning because he had neither the personality of Magsaysay nor the assistance of a strong organization which could have revived the old MPM movement and overcome the Nacionalista and Liberal party machines. In the 1957 election there were no less than five candidates for the presidency: Garcia, Claro M. Recto (who was a strong critic of American policy), José Yulo (nominated by the Liberals), the brother of the deceased Elpidio Quirino, and Manahan. The division of the opposition vote by so many candidates resulted in the return of President Garcia and the majority of his supporters in the Nacionalista Party. The surprise of the election was the success of Diosdado Macapagal, Liberal candidate for the vice-presidency, over the

G

Nacionalista, José B. Laurel. Although a Liberal, Macapagal supported many of the ideas and reforms propounded by Magsaysay and, coming from a family of tenant-farmers in Pampanga, he knew the meaning of poverty. With a good record of honesty in his political career, he was now faced with the same opposition as Magsaysay, not only from the Nacionalista Party but from his own party.

The combination of a Nacionalista president and a Liberal vice-president did not suit Garcia, and he took advantage of the fact that the vice-president of the Philippines does not automatically receive a cabinet portfolio. Garcia decided to ignore Macapagal, and in so doing made not only his biggest political blunder but ensured his own defeat in the next presidential election. Left to himself and with little to do, Macapagal emulated Magsaysay and for the next four years surpassed his record in visiting the barrios, talking to the people in the isolated districts and promising action in redressing their wrongs. Macapagal's personality and appearance soon created an image of a new Magsaysay fired with the need for vigorous leadership to combat increasing corruption and halt the overall downward trend of the economy.

During this period political suspicions had been aroused by a movement to amend the constitution to take care of the social and economic changes since 1935. The first definite attempt at revision was made by President Garcia in 1959 during his 'State of the Nation' message to Congress, which resulted in the creation of a joint Senate-House Committee on Constitutional Amendments. He wanted in particular the election of senators by districts and the synchronization of elections to the two Houses every four years. The Nacionalistas were divided and the House majority floor leader, José M. Aldeguer, who had been a delegate to the 1934–35 convention which had framed the constitution, supported by Senator Quintin Paredes, opposed the national plebiscite. Macapagal, then vice-president, opposed Garcia's plan on the grounds that it was a political move and would not remove corruption.

The failure of the Progressive Party in 1957 had laid the foundation of a new political organization with the leaders and other MPM groups, including Raul S. Manglapus, a former under-secretary of foreign affairs in the Magsaysay administration, and Manuel Manahan. A coalition made up of rebel members of the Nacionalista and Liberal parties, it was named the Grand Alliance. Although supported by numerous groups and a large number of Catholic laymen, only partial success crowned the efforts of the Alliance in the senatorial and local elections of 1959. Manglapus, sometimes called the oldest teenager in politics, saw clearly that their objectives could best be accomplished within the framework of the Liberal Party under Macapagal. With the support of Emmanuel Pelaez, Manuel Manahan and the rest of the Grand Alliance leadership, an understanding was reached with Macapagal a year later. This resulted in the emergence of a new force called the United Opposition of the Liberal Party to fight the Nacionalistas in the 1961 presidential election, with Pelaez as the candidate for the vice-presidency. As the Nacionalistas controlled the administration, had majorities in Congress, held the governorships and in addition received the support of large financial interests including the rich and influential Lopez family, it was generally regarded that President Garcia and the Nacionalista Party would win again. In case anyone remained in doubt, the Nacionalista newspapers did their best to revile Macapagal and his Liberal socio-economic programme.

Against all the odds Macapagal and the Liberal Party, with the support of Manglapus and the United Opposition, swept the poll at the 1961 elections. Emmanuel Pelaez was elected vice-president. Manglapus was also successful and was elected to the Senate, at his third attempt, with the highest popular vote ever given to a candidate for the upper house. Although the Nacionalista Party retained control in the House of Representatives, the Liberals had won six of the eight contested seats for the Senate.

On taking office, Macapagal found that he had inherited from the Garcia administration a national debt not far short of a billion dollars, an empty treasury, widespread evasion of taxes and increasing unemployment. Austerity measures were immediately announced, and Macapagal elaborated the objectives of his administration by defining five goals: to end corruption in the government and the civil service; to improve the rice and corn crops; to launch a bold and massive socio-economic programme; to increase employment; and lastly to introduce a sense of moral values among the people.

Macapagal dealt energetically with the problem of a Nacionalista majority in the House of Representatives and by the end of 1961 had won over sufficient Nacionalista support to give him a majority in the lower house. A constant campaign was waged to beguile provincial officials, in particular governors, persuade them to defect from the Nacionalista Party and give their support to the Liberals who could then obtain control of a majority of the twenty-four seats in the Senate. Though severely criticized in many quarters for trying to destroy the two party system, Macapagal stressed the necessity for the Senate to have a Liberal majority so that the economic programme could be carried through.

In January 1962 Macapagal abolished foreign exchange controls. Further measures were taken to restrict the flow of profits abroad, affecting mostly the Chinese and the Americans who benefited from the provisions of the parity agreement. Decontrol brought about an expected rise in the cost of living, and the real wages of skilled labour quickly deteriorated, while that of unskilled labour remained about the same following a slight increase of some $2\frac{1}{2}$ per cent in wage rates. To alleviate the situation, a bi-partisan Committee on Prices of Prime Commodities was created to combat price rises and was authorized to arrange the importation of foodstuffs at reasonable or subsidized prices.

Despite rising prices and unemployment, the economy moved ahead. The export of sugar benefited from the United States–Russian crisis over Cuba, while copra and other coconut products found a ready market. A move by vested interests to hoard and exploit a shortage of rice was neatly foiled by the government by announcing the sale of rice from strategic stockpiles. A new programme was also outlined by the administration with the object of attracting more foreign capital. Inducements were offered such as tax rebates, tariff protection, tax exemption for reinvested profits and assistance for approved enterprises.

Map of the Philippines

In domestic politics the Liberals were still engaged in their campaign for control of the upper house. They realized their objective early in April 1963 when Senator Ferdinand Marcos took over the Senate presidency from Eulogio Rodriguez. This followed Senator Alejandro's turnabout vote which broke the long-standing deadlock between the two parties. Liberal aims were to strengthen their hold on Congress, and win over more Nacionalistas, defection from one party to another being a normal occurrence in Philippine politics. This is due primarily to the lack of basic ideological differences among the élite who control the principal parties.

President Macapagal's pressing ambition for a working majority in the Senate, and his growing impatience with legalism and the congressional obstruction of his socio-economic policy, brought forth from the opposition charges of dictatorship, personal vindictiveness and disregard for the workings of the constitution. Strong rebuffs had been administered by the supreme court in its decisions that the president could not arbitrarily suspend for an indefinite period the former Governor Perfecto Fayon, Director of the Philippine Virginia Tobacco Administration, and Dr Paulino Garcia, Chairman of the National Science Development Board and a former Health Secretary, despite protests by Macapagal's Secretary of Justice, against the decisions of the tribunal.

The theme of the 'New Era' introduced by Macapagal and expounded to members of the executive branches of the government was that corruption was not something inevitable. Macapagal stressed the importance of dignity, self-sacrifice and simple living. Heated arguments began to permeate the political scene over the proposals of the Land Reform bill which was vigorously challenged by the Nacionalista Party. They claimed that many provisions of the bill were unconstitutional. It was clear that every effort would be made to stop or modify the bill presented to Congress and that, if it were passed, the caciques and other interests would delay implementation by exploiting the ingrained systems of *pabagsak* or bribery and the *compadre* or godfather relationship. Discussions once again were centred around the question of land tenancy and tended to dominate public attention.

In 1961 the Philippines had joined with Thailand and Malaya in setting up the Association of Southeast Asia (ASA). Discussions had gone on for a number of years between the three states following proposals from Bangkok for a form of regional co-operation and President Garcia's specific agreement with Tunku Adbul Rahman of Malaya that the best way to forestall communist activity was to improve economic development and the exchange of cultural and technical activity. However Macapagal was primarily interested in establishing closer relations with Indonesia and in reclaiming for the Sulu heirs the territory of Sabah in North Borneo.

Macapagal's relations with the United States became strained early in 1962 when United States officials seized a shipment of Philippine tobacco; and Harry Stonehill, a wealthy American business man charged with tax evasion, was hastily deported without trial. Severe criticism was levelled at the president's handling of these matters and his open displeasure with the United States. Macapagal cancelled his projected state visit to Washington, changed the Philippine Independence Day from July 4 to June 12 (symbolizing the revolt against Spain) and changed the name of the Manila boulevard commemorating Admiral Dewey to Roxas. This seemed to be an expression of pique at the failure of the United States Congress to pass the $73 million War Damages Claims Bill.

Relations with Malaya had meanwhile become strained and were not improved by Macapagal's granting of asylum to Sheik A. M. Azahari, a politician of mixed Arab–Malay descent and leader of the Brunei People's Party. Thailand attempted to smooth things over, with the result that Tunku Abdul Rahman went to Manila, ostensibly to attend a long overdue ASA conference, with the knowledge that Azahari had been told to leave the Philippines. During the talks with the Tunku, efforts were made by Macapagal to arrange a meeting between the Malayan leader and Sukarno, but the best he could manage was an agreement to hold preliminary discussions at a low level. These were held in April 1963, but in view of the continued hostility of Indonesia towards Malaya little progress was made until Sukarno, during a visit to Japan in early June, suddenly invited the Tunku to see him in Tokyo. Finally Macapagal won approval for his proposal to create a Greater Malay Federation, which eventually became know as Maphilindo, the name being derived from the first syllables of Malaya, the Philippines and Indonesia. Macapagal also pressed for a United Nations' referendum as a concession to the Malayan argument that there was little time left concerning the North Borneo issue.[35]

At the end of July 1963 the anxiously awaited summit conference between Macapagal, Tunku Abdul Rahman and Sukarno took place in Manila barely four weeks after the agreement creating the Federation of Malaysia had been signed in London. The three leaders agreed to collaborate in the future when solving their problems.

On 3 August they signed the Manila Declaration and Manila Accord, setting out the principles of government for Maphilindo. In accordance with the principle of self-determination for North Borneo, they requested the United Nations to ascertain the wishes of the peoples and the British government was asked to enter into peaceful negotiations with the Philippines over the claim to North Borneo. The Manila conference thus ended with all the appearances of friendship and harmonious agreement, though it was obvious that much of the declaration had an Indonesian label.

In September of the same year the United Nations mission announced that a majority of the peoples of North Borneo wished to join the new Federation of Malaysia. The Philippines, following the example of Indonesia, withheld recognition of the Malaysian federation and, after recalling its ambassador, left only a consular office in Kuala Lumpur. Malaysia had no choice but to do likewise and break off diplomatic relations. Macapagal's scheme to prevent the British from transferring sovereignty over North Borneo to Malaysia had completely misfired. Nevertheless the official line was one of *rapprochement* with Djakarta. This reflected a pro-Indonesian policy by the Philippine Foreign Office, causing concern in American and British circles.[36]

On the domestic front the long debate over the Land Reform code only partly ended with the passing on 8 August 1963 of a bill considered the most revolutionary and significant piece of legislation since the reforms of Magsaysay. As expected, strong opposition had been encountered in the Senate, where a special session was called to get the bill enacted, almost every section of it being amended to suit the wishes of the Nacionalista senators. Macapagal continued his campaign in the provinces to win a majority in the Senate elections and almost succeeded. Unfortunately the policy of persuading Nacionalistas to become Liberal had a boomerang effect. Senators Manahan and Antonino turned independent, and Senator Ferdinand Marcos turned to the Nacionalista Party. By the time of the 1965 Presidential campaign there was growing Liberal criticism of Macapagal and Salvador Lopez over their open preference for Indonesia and the exclusion of Malaysia. The pace of Indonesian hostility towards the new Malaysian federation had quickened. Senator Raul Manglapus, who had earlier supported Macapagal through the Grand Alliance, now demanded immediate recognition of Malaysia, and the vice-president, Emmanuel Pelaez, not only opposed the President's policies but announced his intention to join the Nacionalista Party. Seemingly unperturbed, Macapagal brushed aside all argument and a month later, in Djakarta, spoke enthusiastically of the racial ties and culture binding the two countries, acknowledging a Filipino identity with Indonesia.

Considerable diplomatic activity, however, was going on behind the scenes, and the Americans began to use discreet pressure on the Philippine government to ease her official attitude to North Borneo and at the same time to adopt a policy of involvement in Vietnam. Whatever the facts, it is significant that at the 10th meeting of the SEATO ministerial council held in Manila on 13 April 1964 the Philippines gave its vote for support to South Vietnam against communist aggression. A few days earlier Ferdinand Marcos, President of the Senate, and Lorenzo Sumulong, Chairman of the Senate Foreign Affairs Committee, openly subjected Macapagal to strong criticism for giving support to the Indonesian dictator. There was also the news that recent general elections in Malaysia had given the Tunku and his Alliance party a decisive victory. What provoked the President to take action is not known, but shortly afterwards the Secretary of Foreign Affairs, Salvador Lopez, was transferred to another post, and the distinguished journalist and public official, Mauro Mendez, appointed in his place. Though Macapagal still refused to recognize Malaysia, because of the outstanding claim to Sabah in North Borneo, agreement was reached in May to re-establish consular relations.

During this period the final report of the Senate committee on the Stonehill scandal was published and disclosed that high officials of both the Garcia and Macapagal administration had been involved. The Senate majority leader, Arturo Tolentino, brought charges against Macapagal of culpable violation of the constitution and the anti-graft law, and filed impeachment proceedings against him on two counts. The first related to the illegal importation of rice, and the second to the award of $2,250,000 to the Sultan Shipping Line in defiance of a National Economic Council decision to refuse the allocation. Despite the Nacionalista furore over the charges, the general public remained indifferent. This was the second unsuccessful attempt since independence to remove a president by impeachment, the first having been a case against Quirino in 1949.

Macapagal now launched his campaign for re-election. Speaking in Cebu City towards the end of May 1964, he assailed the impeachment proceedings as a Nacionalista bluff and promised that political peace would descend upon the archipelago for the next five years if he retained the presidency. Immediately after this, he received the Liberal Party endorsement. As a result of the endorsement, Macapagal pledged himself to profit by past mistakes and endeavour to become a better president. Financially the Philippines continued to be in difficulty, and dollar reserves were low. The administration was faced with continual delaying tactics in the Nacionalista dominated Senate, and a situation of stalemate existed in Congress over the question of foreign investment.

Members of both the Nacionalista and Liberal parties expressed their concern at Sukarno's developing ambitions, and Macapagal made new efforts to bring Tunku Abdul Rahman and the Indonesian leader together. In June, Sukarno and Tunku met in Tokyo, with Macapagal in attendance, but it was impossible to bridge the difference between Malaysia and Indonesia, and the meeting collapsed

94

after two days. At the same time events in Vietnam were becoming a cause of anxiety. In accordance with the decisions of the last SEATO meeting in Manila, Macapagal received the consent of Congress in July 1964 for his bill to grant economic and technical aid to South Vietnam.

A few weeks later the clash between American and North Vietnamese vessels in the Gulf of Tonking and the bombing of bases showed clearly that the United States was committed to military escalation in Asia, a policy which began to arouse concern in many countries, not least in the Philippines. Almost simultaneously, Indonesian guerrillas had landed by air and sea in Malaysia. On 3 September 1964 the Tunku declared a state of emergency.

Macapagal took every opportunity to calm the situation and prevent further deterioration in relations with the Tunku. In October, Salvador Lopez warned the United Nations that the claim to North Borneo would be placed on the agenda of the General Assembly—unless Malaysia agreed to submit the case to the World Court. Lopez was quickly repudiated by Macapagal, who declared that the Philippines had no intention of bringing the matter before the United Nations. Macapagal deplored the landings of Indonesian guerrillas in Malaysia and said that mediation could not continue unless they were withdrawn. This indicated a big change in policy and probably reflected not only the anxiety felt in political circles in Manila but also the efforts made by the Thai Foreign Minister, Thanat Khoman, to keep ASA alive and strengthen economic development in Southeast Asia.

The Philippine economy was still in a state of inflation and of seemingly little concern to the politicians who blocked proposed tax laws in the legislature. Holdings of foreign exchange had, however, increased because of higher export receipts and monetary restrictions imposed by the Central Bank. Exporters were still hampered by the requirement that 20 per cent of the export proceeds be converted at the official rate of two pesos to the dollar and paid to the Central Bank. The cost of living had risen by nearly 10 per cent. Though employment in both the manufacturing and allied sectors had increased at the expense of agriculture, the overall rate of unemployment continued to be acute, with unrest and bitterness developing within the few trade unions. New investment in industry was sluggish, and many schemes of social reconstruction had collapsed due to a lack of funds and implementation, in some cases caused by political obstruction. The national debt showed a large increase. Despite the creation a year earlier of the post of Presidential Assistant on Housing, construction was less than 10 per cent of requirement. Figures issued in November 1964 indicated that the Philippines had one of the lowest investments in housing in the world. Criticism of the president gathered momentum despite factionalism. To the outside observer it appeared that Macapagal, overburdened with numerous trivial public engagements, not only prevented his senior colleagues from sharing in governmental responsibilities but actually succeeded in removing all possible rivals and opponents from the administration.

The year 1965 began with feverish preparations for the coming presidential election. Senator Raul Manglapus organized once again a third party, called the Party for Philippine Progress, with the support of a number of former MPM members who were anxious to bring new ideas and attitudes to old problems. The Liberal Party organization had been enlarged to embrace a number of associated movements, such as the Macapagal-Roxas or MR movement. The president was personally engaged on country-wide electioneering campaigns. Conscious of the criticism in commercial quarters concerning the economic situation, Macapagal and his administration continued nevertheless in the belief that its record, even if not spectacular, would appeal to the mass of voters against the past record, promises and ambiguities of the Nacionalistas. Foreign affairs have never been decisive issues in Philippine elections. The struggles going on in Malaysia and Vietnam had already receded into the background. Visiting a number of neglected towns in the Visayas and Mindanao, Macapagal stressed in his speeches that the slow pace of economic progress was caused by bitter and partisan opposition. He urged farmers to rouse themselves from the lethargy which years of cacique power had forced upon them and to help the administration implement the Land Reform programme.

In Congress continuous discussion was going on concerning amendments to the Constitution on the grounds that the original document had been drafted and promulgated at a time when the archipelago was still under American sovereignty and could not, therefore, express the true will and purpose of the Filipinos. Nationalist feeling had been aroused by the knowledge that American companies were bringing pressure to bear on the government over the Retail Trade Act and the fight to end the monopoly of the pharmacentical industry. These business interests opposed the establishment of new industries that might compete with their own enterprises in the Philippines.

Senator Ferdinand Marcos now emerged as the victor of the struggle within the Nacionalista Party for the nomination as presidential candidate. Senator Fernando Lopez obtained the vice-presidential nomination, while Emanuel Pelaez had to be content to be one of eight senatorial candidates. As the day of the election drew nearer the parties began to excel themselves in the vilification of each other's personalities. The Nacionalistas, led by the Senate majority leader, Arturo M. Tolentino, charged Macapagal and his administration with criminal neglect of hospitals, transportation and the basic agricultural industries. Marcos came out against involvement in Vietnam, as this would constitute a new phase in foreign policy. The Liberals, in turn, charged the Nacionalistas with obstruction of bills designed to boost agricultural production and attacked them for supporting Lopez and the strong-arm methods of vested interests like the Manila Electric Company.

Political capital as well as acrimonious criticisms were made by both Marcos and Macapagal over the support for the Nacionalistas by the militant Iglesia ni Kristo or Church of Christ Movement and the unofficial support for the Liberals by the Catholics. This provoked an outburst from the leaders of the largest trade unions, who considered the Iglesia ni Kristo an open enemy of trade unionism and completely dominated by Felix Manalo, who had little interest for the social problems confronting the country.

The third political party, led by Senator Raul Manglapus, with the support of Manuel Manahan, attacked both Liberals and Nacionalistas

97

for their waste of public money on political propaganda and the buying of votes. Considerable emphasis was given to the argument that Liberals and Nacionalistas were more or less two factions of the same party and supported equally by the same vested interests.

Although Manglapus, Manahan and a few others in the movement were known and respected, the Party for Philippine Progress was practically unknown to the great mass of people. Without large funds and influential support it was unable to present a real threat to the main contestants, especially as elections in the Philippines have hitherto been more of a popularity contest among the different candidates rather than a choice between rival programmes.

The Commission on Elections, popularly known as Comelec, was fully engaged in its capacity as overseer of the electoral campaigns and did its best to ensure a fair and peaceful polling day. On 9 November 1965, 75 per cent of the registered voters elected President Ferdinand Marcos, and Fernando Lopez as Vice-President.[37] The Nacionalistas had come to power, but the Liberals retained a majority in the House of Representatives, while the Senate appeared to be divided up in such a way that checks and balances would be exploited by minority groupings.

The tasks confronting the new president had been complicated by Macapagal making last-minute appointments of his supporters to government positions and instructing them not to resign. In foreign affairs Marcos was faced with the choice of withdrawing or insisting on the claim to North Borneo, despite a flat rejection by Tunku Abdul Rahman. News coming out of Indonesia indicated growing opposition to the policies of Sukarno. Vietnam and the participation of the Philippines in the war was a question which had not been solved, though at a news conference in November Marcos had said he was against sending Filipino soldiers to that area. At home he was faced with national frustration over the country's economic affairs, with widespread poverty, crime and smuggling increasing at an alarming rate. Marcos promised to give heroic leadership for a republic in a crisis.[38]

7   Society, religion and culture

THE PHILIPPINES is a country of diversity. Regionalism exists in manners and customs as well as in temperament and the use of dialect. Spanish provides the basis for a large number of common words and is still spoken among the older traditionalist class. English, the lingua franca of the archipelago, is a legacy of the years of American rule. The thorny question of Tagalog as a national and third language, now known as Pilipino, is fiercely discussed. In the ordinary home the local dialect takes pride of place.³⁹

The social structure is typical of Asia, with kinship ties based on a system that includes all relatives of the father and mother. Children are taught filial obedience to elders in a family environment that strongly conditions their attitude to life. Responsibility is defined and older children look after their younger brothers and sisters. If the father dies, the eldest son takes over his duties, putting aside considerations of his own personal happiness. Traditionally decisions regarding marriage, career, disposal of property, personal relationships etc, are made according to the wishes of one's family. Beyond the immediate family the individual has wide latitude in choosing those with whom he will develop a close contact, since, through both parents, he will probably have an enormous number of relatives. Christian Filipinos extend this pattern to include those not directly related by blood or marriage as a form of ritual kinship. When the occasion is baptism, confirmation or marriage, godparents are chosen who assume the responsibility for religious instruction, and in certain circumstances provide support and material welfare.

Fully aware of the security that the family can give, many Filipinos establish a family business and this provides jobs for their relatives. This system, common in Asia and Latin America, has given certain families a dominant position in politics and trade. A Filipino helps his relatives and intimate friends partly as a duty, partly with the expectation that he will be helped in time of need. Consequently many of the problems common in the Western world connected with old age and infirmity have not hitherto existed in the Philippines. It is still common for many generations of the same family to live together under the same roof. No old-age homes are found in the Philippines. Though marriage brings new responsibilities for newly-weds it does not change their ties or obligations to their respective families. One's obligations are lifelong. Everyone is involved, whether it be financial help or a solution to a family argument. A man who mistreated his wife would be faced immediately by her irate father and brothers. The continuous support given to a wife by her family and kin is one of the reasons for the strong position of women in Filipino society. She is the central figure in the family, wife, mother, treasurer and disburser of funds. In accordance with the traditional Filipino custom, now a part of the Civil Code, the property which a women brings to marriage is her own and she may do as she like over its disposition. Enjoying an equal status with her husband, she nevertheless gives him the illusion that he is lord and master of his household. Although she accepts a form of double morality, the males being allowed freedoms denied the female members of her family, her informal influence in society often affects the economic and political affairs of the country. At election time personal ties to candidates are more important than political issues.

While Filipinos know how to live together within the family circle, they often find it difficult to co-operate effectively outside the home. They have difficulty in seeing that the overall interest of the community is of importance. Robert Fox has written, 'the manner in which life in the Philippines centres on the family and household is vividly illustrated by the concept of sanitation tradition-ally held. Thus, the dwellings and yard are always clean while the community as a whole—roads, areas between households and so forth—does not appear so. Persons feel obligated to clean on the area of their own households, and the absence of effective community-wide organizations inhibit programmes of community sanitation'.[40] Another obstacle to wider co-operation among the people is the basic inability of the Filipino to accept or make criticism. He is super-sensitive to anything affecting his pride or dignity. This racial trait, typical of the Malay, is commonly known as *Hiya*. The frankness of foreigners is sometimes tolerated but never comprehended. The Filipinos have a strong sense of hospitality, politeness and modesty, closely related to their self-esteem. They are generally bad losers, and will offer all sorts of reasons for defeat. For instance an unsuccessful political candidate usually accuses the winner of fraud, cheating and unfair practices. These national traits may give the impression that the average Filipino is fickle, untrustworthy, temperamental, proud and lazy. However, one must beware of such generalizations; in reality the opposite may often apply. Many writers have called the Filipinos indolent, but it is worth remembering what José Rizal wrote in 1890, 'the causes of the supposed indolence of the Filipinos originate not so much from the climate as from the lack of stimuli to work as a result of the political system under which they live'.[41]

The people are inherently religious and, regardless of denomination, religion is a strong factor in determining and conditioning the daily life of almost every individual. This factor was exploited by the Spanish missionaries who, from the time of Legazpi, worked hard to spread the Christian faith. Although many missionairies fostered discontent and hostility among sections of the local population, they played an important part in the planning of early towns and cities, and the building of churches and parochial schools. With the spread of the Christian religion, Catholicism became an integral part of the national life, though diluted with pre-Spanish traditional beliefs and ritual. Religion is more family-centred than church-centred, and many people have household shrines and own carved wooded statues of saints, which are carried in rural processions. Church attendance and other religious obligations are considered a family affair, with the female members assuming these duties for the entire family. Catholicism has a strong hold on the bulk of the population, especially the women, because from the beginning it was not only a new religion but brought European dress, customs, music and ideas.

Many religious sects exist which merge animistic beliefs with traditional Catholic practices. Some religious groups consider Rizal as a god, while others believe him to have been endowed with supernatural powers. All these sects, appeal to a sense of patriotism just as religious concepts have been part of almost every mass movement, including the Hukbalahap guerrillas and the fanatical Lapiang Malaya led by Tatang de los Santos. In 1967 this movement demanded the resignation of President Marcos, and ordered the army to march on his official residence. The police and constabulary intervened and attacked the headquarters of the Lapiang Malaya in Pasay City, killing thirty Lapiang Malaya followers, wounding many more and imprisoning the remainder.[42]

After the American occupation of the Philippines in 1898, Catholicism was deprived of its status as the official religion. Nevertheless, despite the encouragement of Protestant missions by the Americans and the emergence of other sects belonging to the Free Church, Catholicism maintained an influence in society and politics. Divorce is not allowed, and Catholics in the government and in Congress would never allow the introduction of birth control. Also there are many Catholic women who take an active part in political affairs and hold important positions in the administration. The Jesuits have always had influence on education and scientific research and have given technical training to many young Filipinos anxious to enter industry or the professions.

The Republic of the Philippines is today a country in transition, ranging from the most primitive to the ultra-modern, with forms of artistic expression revealing a rich and varied cultural heritage from the Chinese, Japanese, Arab, Hindu and Malay contacts before and during the early Spanish period. The concept of a national art, however, did not exist until the late sixteenth century when the archipelago had become economically and politically united. From this period onwards the Spaniards placed more emphasis on gracious living. Art in the Philippines may be considered as being divided into two categories, Christian and the non-Christian. Christian art found expression in the beautification and adornment of churches, mostly accomplished with the help of Chinese craftsmen and Filipinos. The Spaniards also introduced European styles of costume and furniture which were adapted to suit the climatic conditions in the islands. The heavy, decorative dress worn by Spanish women gradually gave way to a lightweight blouse having full embroidered sleeves and a skirt with wide black stripes called the 'Maria Clara', the forerunner of the mestiza or terno dress with large butterfly sleeves made of stiff netting. The origin of the Philippine contribution to native dress can be traced to the early Malayan costume of a long one-piece plaid wrap-around skirt topped by the long-sleeved jacket worn in southern Luzon and the Visayas. Another development was the replacement of the heavily starched ruff of the Spanish dress with a neckpiece called the Panuelo, made from loosely woven fibre and embellished with delicate embroidery.

The male version of the Maria Clara is a shirt made from native cloth, elegantly embroidered and worn outside the trousers. Known as the Barong Tagalog, it has become the national attire, worn on formal occasions by the majority of men from the president downwards. It is characterized by its design and embroidery and the *pina* cloth hand-woven from pineapple fibres or *jusi*, a soft material hand-woven from raw silk thread.

The first Filipino paintings were of patron saints and scenes of the Passion, copied from engravings and paintings belonging to the religious orders. Slowly over the years the beginnings of a secular art emerged, and by the end of the eighteenth century portrait painting had the patronage of the wealthy ruling class. Although there were already a small number of talented painters, the first to gain public recognition was a mestizo, Damian Domingo, who had considerable influence with the Spanish authorities. With their support he was able to open the first art school in Manila in 1815. This was later taken over by the Spanish administration, named the

Academia de Bellas Artes, and provided with Spanish instructors.

More frequent contact with Europe, following the opening of the Suez Canal in 1869, enabled Filipino artists to study the work of European painters, resulting in a change of style and composition. A number of young Filipino painters—Isidro Arceo, Antonio Asuncion, Lorenzo Guerrero, Eusebio Santos and Miguel Zaragoza —became renowned for their work. Among the Filipinos who went to Spain to study, and campaign for reforms and eventual independence, were the artists Juan Luna and Felix Resurreccion Hidalgo. They were the first Filipino artists to gain international fame with their respective paintings *Spoliarum* and *Christian Women Exposed to the Populace*, which won first and second prize at the Madrid Exposition of Fine Arts in 1884. The outbreak of Spanish–American hostilities in 1898 led to the closing of many schools and colleges, including the Academia de Bellas Artes. After the Americans had occupied the Philippines the academy was reopened in 1909 as a part of the newly established University of the Philippines.

With Jorge Pineda in the forefront, the illustrators of this era were now emerging as artists in their own right. Pineda drew numerous scenes of country life for local periodicals. By 1920 another illustrator and painter, named Fernando Amorsolo, had attracted attention with his bold use of colour and his Impressionist style, probably influenced by the Spanish painter, Joaquin Sorolla, and the Swede, Anders Zorn. Much of his work portrayed aspects of rural life. Amorsolo taught and influenced a whole generation of painters, and even today traces of his style are evident in magazine illustrations and in the work of young painters. Around 1930 he was challenged by Victorio Edades, a Filipino freshly returned from studies in the United States. At first Edades was ridiculed and misunderstood, but he was soon joined by other painters such as Carlos Francisco, Diosdado Lorenzo, Galo Ocampo and Ricarte Puruganan. Their work was an inspiration to other Filipino artists and they greatly stimulated the intellectual and emotional range of Filipino painting.[43]

Philippine architecture, prior to the arrival of the Spaniards in the sixteenth century, was characterized by the pile house which consisted of a square or rectangular living space raised two to six feet above the ground in the form of a hut, the size of which depended not only on the wealth of the owner but also on the organization and status of the family within the community. Cool, adaptable and easily constructed from wood, bamboo and palm leaf, this Nipa Hut is still the prototype of most dwellings in the archipelago, and is easily modified to local conditions. In the southern islands the style has been strongly influenced by Muslim culture and the introduction of the features of the mosque. Naturally the Spanish conquest and the zeal and power of the missionaries was a major contribution to the growth of architecture in the Philippines. Villages and towns were built with a judicious blending of indigenous and Spanish design, distinguished by the placing of the church and timber or stone buildings, around a rectangular plaza. The design of houses were inspired by Antillan architecture with a lower part constructed of stone and heavy staircases leading to the projecting upper part of timber which formed the living quarters. Usually the roofs were tiled. The threat of tremors and earthquakes made architects concentrate on eliminating the causes of collapse.

In the early days churches were built of nipa and bamboo, but were replaced by more permanent buildings following the introduction of brick and adobe. European designs were used and modified and to suit local conditions. By the end of the seventeenth century rich baroque architecture with its characteristic sculptured façade had made its appearance. Many designs were modified by Chinese and Filipino artisans who introduced their own ideas. A school of architectural decoration slowly emerged as a result of native skill in carving and a sense of ornamentation. One could call it a mestizo style, a compound of Oriental and Western ideas often resulting in a miscellany of Chinese lions, demon figures, crocodiles and coconut palms alongside contrasting forms of romanesque, gothic and baroque decoration. Though this can give the onlooker a feeling of bewilderment, one can marvel at the technical virtuosity displayed and accept it as an inevitable stage in the continuing development of a style typically Filipino. Buildings where one can find this sort of decoration are the ruins of the monastery of

Guadalupe at Makati, Rizal, the San Augustin Church in Manila, the Santa Ana Church in Manila.

A revival of European architectural design occurred during the nineteenth century and continued during the early years of the American occupation. By the beginning of the 1920s changes began to take place in Manila with the introduction of massive concrete structures to house government offices. Classic in form, grandiose in conception, with graceful columns and ornamental façades. The new style made a strong impact on the young Filipino architects who saw it as a manifestation of dignity and wealth. Hospitals, schools, hotels, stores, apartments, theatres, and office buildings were built according to American concepts. A typically Filipino style had been forgotten. Apart from the introduction of modern functionalism the period between the two World Wars was one of retrogression. However, intensive urban development and reconstruction after independence presented a challenge for Filipino architects. Their skill in adapting reinforced concrete frames, glass and wood to make buildings suitable for a tropical climate, and in blending old and new architectural concepts, is typified by the work of Pablo Antonio, Leandro Locsin, Carlos Arguelles, Cesar Concio and Angel Nakpil. Visitors to Manila can see examples of their work in the Capitan Luis Gonzaya Building, the National Press Club, and the Chapel of the Holy Sacrifice at the University of the Philippines, Quezon City.

The non-Christian minorities such as the Muslims in the south and the Ifugaos in northern Luzon have had a traditional type of sculpture, going back to the pre-Spanish era. The emphasis is on woodcarving and metalwork influenced by religious beliefs and ritual. With the coming of the Spaniards and the introduction of Christianity, the local artisans learned the basic elements of European sculpture and attained distinction for their exquisite wood-carvings of religious figures, and their embellishment of churches and shrines. Sculpture in the Philippines has been closely wedded to religious architecture, but until recently has not had any significance as a separate art-form. However, there has been an increasing appreciation of contemporary sculpture which has ranged, like painting, from the most orthodox to the extreme abstract, the latter in general indistinguishable from work seen in the United States, Japan, France and elsewhere. Among the sculptors who have achieved recognition are Veloso Abueva and José Alcantara, with their effective use of native adobe, stone, wood and copper. Nevertheless sculpture, as an indigenous art-form, is today still in its infancy in the Philippines.

Studies of pre-Spanish history show that the early Filipinos were great lovers of music and fond of singing and dancing. The diverse cultural background which emerged as a result of Hindu-Malayan, Chinese and Indonesian influences has given the Filipino a rare instinct for musical rhythm and a natural gift for expressing himself in dance. Similarly, poems have been made into songs, which the people readily dance to and sing. Many of the oldest songs, familiar today, may be classified as lullabies (*hinli*), songs of the wayfayer (*dalit*), marriage songs (*diona*), war songs (*kumintang*), song of sorrow (*lumbay*), and love songs (*kundiman*). Numerous other songs were sung by the people when they worked in the home, in the fields, rowed their river boats (*bangkas*) or went to sea. Local communities had their own collection of songs, dances and musical instruments.

Many of these songs and dances can still be found among the Muslims and non-Christian minorities. Great skill is displayed in using native flutes and percussion instruments, such as the kulintangan, which is a graduated set of gongs similar to the Javanese camelan and usually about three feet long. Among the stringed instruments the kudyapi, which is made of wood, resembles an elongated guitar with two strings. The Filipinos' love of music and dancing was carefully exploited by the Spanish missionaries, who used sacred music as an integral part of their church services. Many of the Augustinian and Franciscan friars were accomplished musicians and instructed their converts in composing with more developed musical scales and concepts. The Filipinos had little difficulty in assimilating Spanish influences in music while retaining their native style, and soon they were dancing the *habañera*, *fandango* and *rigodon* and singing Spanish songs in their own graceful and inimitable manner. The Church encouraged the development of religious music, and in 1742 a school was established in Manila. By the end of the eighteenth century a number of societies had been formed to foster the arts and musical drama, and with the infiltration of musical ideas from Europe and Latin America a steady development could be noted. Folk-dancing began to take on new characteristics and today many show traces of Spanish, English, French, German and American influence.

During the nineteenth century Spanish musical comedy (*zarzuela*) and Italian opera were introduced in the Philippines. After 1892 many of the Filipino composers and writers began to write in the style of the zarzuela, and before the turn of the century the first native operetta called *Banduggong Panaginip* had been produced with a libretto by Pedro Paterno and music by Ladislao Bonua. The popularity of the zarzuela was basically due to the language used and the subject matter and became a potent medium for satire and and social protest against the Spanish régime. This often resulted in the arrest of the authors and producer.

With the American occupation came the immediately popular ragtime and jazz, which spread rapidly throughout the islands at the expense of indigenous creative activity. The popularity of this music was fostered by the growth of cinema and broadcasting and the introduction of the gramophone. Interest in native and classical music waned, though a number of prominent musicians and singers attempted unsuccessfully to revive some interest. The Manila Symphony Orchestra Society was founded in 1932, but little was done to extend its field of influence beyond that city. The appeal of westernization and the impact of American culture satisfied the Filipino's traditional love of show and pleasure. It was not until the Japanese occupation during the Second World War that significant changes took place.

Japan endeavoured from the outset to persuade the Filipinos that she had come as a liberator and that independence would follow if they would co-operate in the establishment of the Great East Asia Co-Prosperity Sphere. The cinema and schools were utilized in propoganda to eliminate American influence in favour of Japanese culture and a return to an Asian way of life. Fully aware of the importance of the theatre and music, the Japanese encouraged a revival of native culture. In 1942 the first all-Filipino concert was given by the New Symphony Orchestra conducted by Francisco Santiago. Other concerts were organized giving an opportunity to a number of Filipino composers who included Liwanag Cruz, Ramon Tapales and Felipe de Leon. Folk-dancing attracted attention once again, while the theatre, especially in Manila, flourished with entertainment for all ages ranging from vaudeville to serious drama, For the people it provided an escape from the reaility of the Japanese military occupation.[4]

After the war, creative musical and theatrical activity declined as American films and light music again flooded the cultural scene. Dance bands and popular entertainment soon took ascendancy over creative activity in the performing arts. However, today there is a growing interest in the development of native culture; and the success of the Bayanihan Folk Arts Centre in Manila which performs abroad, has stirred the national conscience.

The large import of foreign films, mostly American, has been a factor in restricting the growth of the Philippine film industry which, hitherto, has not exploited local talent or the wealth of available material to project a national image. Though the films now shown in the Philippines have greatly improved, they reveal cheap commercial tendencies and are in general devoid of any real artistic merit. It is only fair to state that little support or encouragement has been given by the government towards the making of films of quality and of documentary value. There has also been little use of the cinema as a medium for instruction and furthering technical knowledge. Whether the future expansion of television, at the moment confined to the big cities, will bring about any improvement, is a matter for speculation.

Much of the literature of the pre-Spanish period has either been lost or was destroyed by the early Spanish missionaries as idolatrous. The ancient system of writing with points on bark or palm leaves, using an alphabet of seventeen letters, was discouraged, and the romanization of the script by the friars has almost brought about its eradication. Today only the Mangyan tribe in Mindoro and the Tagbanuas of Palawan are known to use the old alphabet. Fortunately a considerable amount of oral literature has been handed down from generation to generation in the form of folklore and epic poems. These include the *Darangan* of the Lanao Muslims, which is a collection of tales about the exploits of Maranaw heroes; the epics of the Ifugaos, known as *Hudhud* and *Alim;* and the Ilocano's popular narrative called *Biag-ni-Lam-ang*, which in its present form gives a remarkable picture of life in the Ilocos region in pre-Spanish times as well as a rich sociological panorama of pagan practices and the impact of Christian-rites and beliefs.

In many a village or barrio traditional stories are still narrated, often with a moral or lesson, in moments of joy or sadness or simply as a pastime. Sometimes it may be a tongue-twisting witticism or proverb; more often than not a fable with a title like, *The Origin of the Stars*, *The First Ancestors*, *The Sniffing Dogs*, *Man's Three Friends* and *Juan Tamad*, the legendary folk hero who gains his ends, unscrupulously or otherwise, with little effort.

The first printing press using engraved woodblocks was introduced by the Dominican Fathers towards the end of the sixteenth century. The first book to be printed was the prayer book *Doctrina Christiana* in two editions, one Spanish and Tagalog and the other Chinese. A number of artisans were trained by the friars as printers and engravers. The Chinese edition of the *Doctrina Christiana* was printed by the Chinese engraver Keng Yong, who had been converted to the Catholic faith and took the name Juan de Vera. Together with the Dominican friars he is reputed to have devised movable type. The first book printed with movable type was *Libro de las Excellencias del Rosario de Nuestra Senora y Sus Misterios*. In 1610 the printing press was transferred to Abucay, Bataan, where, for reasons unknown, the work was taken over by a Filipino artisan named Tomas Pinpin, who was one of the first to write in Tagalog.

The development of vernacular literature during the next two hundred years produced little of literary significance. It consisted mainly of religious works, books and pamphlets on morals, miracle plays, and some metrical romances, all reflecting the strong influence of the church and the form of education given by the missionaries. Then, in the middle of the nineteenth century, a dramatic change occurred as a result of the political events in Spain and the infiltration of European ideas and themes which inspired the Tagalog poet Francisco Baltazar, better known as Balagtas, who wrote an outstanding metrical romance called *Florante at Laura*. It contained revolutionary implications so cleverly camouflaged that it passed the Spanish censorship. A new, bold literature now appeared written in both Spanish and Tagalog in which poetry, essays, and novels, were written to examine the aspirations and problems of the Filipinos. Newspapers like *La Esperanza*, *El Diario de Manila* and *La Ilustracion Filipina* appeared. Despite censorship, these provided an outlet for a number of versatile writers.

Prominent poets of this period were José Cruz or Huseng Sisiw, remembered for *Clarita*, *Segismundo* and *Adela at Florante*, and Pedro A. Paterno, the first Filipino to publish his poems in book form (*Sampaguitas y Poesias Varias*) in Madrid in 1880. The Filipinos' struggle for freedom was beautifully expressed in José Palma's poem *Filipinas*, which nowadays is sung as the national anthem to the music of J. Felipe. Many patriotic students and writers contributed to the propaganda movement in Spain and the periodical *La Solidaridad*, founded by Lopez Jaena. This was later edited by an ardent nationalist and brilliant journalist called Marcelo H. del Pilar, who wrote a whole series of articles in Tagalog. Other prominent writers to emerge during this era were Mariano Ponce, José Ma. Panganiban, Antonio Luna and Isabelo de los Reyes. Rizal overshadowed them all as the most distinguished writer of the revolutionary period and a penetrating critic of the Spanish régime and the weaknesses of his fellow Filipinos. Educated by the Jesuits in Manila, he displayed a great breadth of intellectual interest and had rather the outlook of an European humanist. Anxious for fundamental political and social reforms. Rizal reveals these aims throughout his writing, most of which was done in Europe in support for the Propagandist movement in Spain. Though he wrote many essays for *La Solidaridad*, his most important work was unquestionably his great social novels, *Noli me Tangere* and *El Filibusterismo*, published in Europe in 1887 and 1891 respectively. These vividly exposed the humiliation and suffering of his fellow countrymen under Spanish rule.

Rizal, though remembered for his novels, lives mostly in the memory of his fellow Filipinos because of his poetical masterpiece *Ultimo Adios* or *The Last Farewell*, composed in his prison cell before his execution. Written in Spanish, later translated into many other languages, this poem reveals in the first stanza the soul and purpose of the man who became a national hero:

> *Farewell, dear Fatherland, clime of the sun caress'd*
> *Pearl of the Orient Seas, our Eden lost!*
> *Gladly now I go to give thee this faded life's best*
> *And were it brighter, fresher or more blest,*
> *Still would I give it thee, nor count the cost.*

After the annexation of the archipelago by the United States, the fervent sentiment of nationalism in literature continued to express itself in poetry and the zarzuela. Notable are the works of Severino Reyes, Lope Santos, Pedro Paterno, Faustina Aguilar, Aurelio Tolentino and Patricia Mariano, to mention a few. The use of Tagalog increased in popularity, and before the end of the 1920s a number of magazines appeared in which the best Tagalog poems and stories were published. Many Filipino writers, however, continued to write in Spanish. Some of them, including Fernando Ma. Guerrero, Claro Recto, Manuel Bernabe and Joaquin Balmori, produced their best work during this period.

Gradually the impact of American journalism, the introduction of English, and the rapid diffusion of education began to be felt. By 1922, a number of writers began to write short stories instead of essays and poems. In 1930 Maximo Kalaw, a political philospher and essayist, wrote his only novel, in English, called *The Filipino Rebel*, which dealt with the social and political implications of the American occupation in a style reminiscent of Rizal. During the Commonwealth period, President Quezon took steps to stimulate the growth of a national literature in English, Tagalog and Spanish, and a

112

number of literary competitions were held. In 1938 Rafael Palma won the competition for the best biography with his entry on José Rizal, written in Spanish and better known through the English translation *The Pride of the Malay Race*. Other competitions were held in 1940 and 1941 under the auspices of the Philippine Writers League, with prizes for the best writing in the three official languages Topics of discussion were moral decadence, the national conscience and social problems. Foremost among writers of this period was Salvador P. Lopez, whose essays entitled *Literature and Society* not only won the Commonwealth Award for Literature but provoked, and still provoke, critical debate in literary circles. The short story became fully developed as the result of contributions from such writers as José Garcia Villa, Manuel Arguilla and Arturo Rotor.[45]

After the Japanese occupation in 1942 and the suppression of the press, many authors stopped writing, and literary activity stagnated despite Japanese efforts to impress the Filipinos with their own Asian culture. However, magazines in Tagalog, such as *Liwayway*, became popular and even now continue to increase their circulation. The absence of American films during the war revived interest in the theatre, and the drama became once again a vehicle for expressing national ideals. This revival became particularly strong following the liberation, and was characterized by a preference for drama based on Filipino themes. A number of well-organized theatrical groups got started and stimulated the interest of rural communities in the theatre. The enthusiasm displayed by these groups, made up mostly of amateurs, emphasized the need for a professional theatre and the government's failure to provide any real support.[46]

As an incentive a number of play-writing competitions have been held by associations such as the Arena Theatre, Palanca, the Philippine Mental Health Association and the University of the Philippines Drama Club, but the complex language problem complicates the choice of medium. Plays in English are seldom performed Writers who have improved the standard of play-writing include Carlos Romulo, with his short satire *Daughters for Sale;* Claro Recto, whose tragedy *Shadow and Solitude* was written in Spanish and translated into English by Nick Joaquin; and Antonio Bayot, with his social drama *Rigodon*.

The revival of Filipino literature in English during the post-war period is best shown in the writings of R. Zuleta de Costa, Carlos Romulo, Carlos Bulosan, Emigdio Enriquez, Celso Al. Carunungan, N. V. Gonzales, Nick Joaquin and Bienvenido Santos. A promising newcomer to the literary scene is Linda Ty Casper, whose novel, *The Peninsulars*, published in 1964, is a competent work in the best tradition of the Philippines. The present undistinguished state of literature in the archipelago probably results from the confusion regarding the use of Pilipino as a national language. The number of people who read Tagalog exceeds those who read English, whereas Filipino writers, for the most part, write in English.

Book publishing has remained very limited, and with the exception of Manila and the large cities, little has been done to encourage reading or to create a demand for books. Lending libraries are few and scattered. Consequently not many books are available in rural areas. Despite the improved facilities for education, reading is not widespread as a recreation. The reading habits of the majority of people have been formed by inadequate schooling, the commercial exploitation of comic books, and a lurid press. There is also the attraction of the cinema, commercial radio, and in large cities American-style television. Consequently much of the apparent distaste for serious reading is often the outcome of an acceptance of Western commercialism and the weaknesses in the public and private school systems. The rapid development of commercialized entertainment and sporting activities have also retarded the transition from an oral culture to a more literate society.

The average Filipino, whether from the town or country areas, enjoys sport and gambling, and is not averse to a lively debate, especially in the rural districts where the barrio stores provide a forum for arguing about political issues or the varied problems of the farming community. Although the people are becoming more interested in competitive sports like boxing, swimming, tennis, baseball and basketball (at present the leading sport of the archipelago), the vast majority still find their recreation in watching cockfighting, which has for centuries been popular with all classes of Filipinos. Almost every municipality has its official *gallera*, where cockfighting is allowed only on Sundays and public holidays, starting early in the morning and lasting until sunset. Cockfights take place in an atmosphere of feverish excitement as family fortunes are often won or lost. The desire to gamble is very strong, and every night after dark the roulette wheels spin, the dice roll and the cards are shuffled. In Manila the quiniela version of Jai-alai, popular in the United States, Mexico and Cuba, draws large crowds. There are many native games, the most popular being a ball game called *Sipa*, and a form of fencing called *Arnis*, in which rattan staffs are used.

The Filipinos have a remarkable sense of make-believe. Life is a constant source of fun and the urge to be merry is seen in the innumerable fiestas, where expense is of secondary importance, to eating, drinking, listening to brass bands, watching beauty contests and colourful religious processions with long lines of candle bearers and, gaily decorated floats. Almost every town has a patron saint whose day will be celebrated locally with a fiesta. During these festivities the Filipino hostess is never surprised to see strangers in her home. People continually wander in and out, and for the sake of prestige, she must prepare her best food. The poor family who can match the lavishness of a wealthy neighbour achieves status in the Philippine sense as far as the neighbourhood is concerned. Success is triumph, even if it results in lasting debt. What does matter is that the successful family has had its moment of glory. This extravagance is a trait of all Filipinos. The Filipino, of all classes, ignores the future and wants most of all to escape from the drudgery of daily life and the problems of inequality between the priviledged and the bulk of the people who make a meager living, hardly at subsistence level. As mentioned before, this is a society, undermined by political corruption at all levels, where people display an ingenious evasion of traditional ethics and law. The Filipino hears or reads daily about underpaid workers, the use of inferior raw materials by manufacturers who mislead the public and bribe government inspectors. He knows about the sons of the wealthy who often commit crimes, and about the rise of smuggling as one of the country's biggest industries, about police complicity, etc. Still the man in the street maintains, 'A smart guy has prestige. If you have money, influence or in the government, you can get away with anything including murder! To be smart is all right—just so long you do not get caught!'

One word in Tagalog is sufficient to express the general attitude of a large number of people—*Lamangan*—which means 'by hook or by crook to get on top'. Perhaps the reason behind this attitude is the knowledge that the family represents to the Filipino the only source of love, sustenance and security. He does not see any harm in putting his relatives or friends in jobs which might be better filled with strangers. If times are bad and his family is in need, he is likely to do anything, even if it means breaking the law, to get money. Lamangan explains a lot about the Filipinos. Politicians with family obligations have to satisfy an even wider circle of supporters who clamour for work and assistance.

Headlines in the press mean little to the average wage earner. He is fully occupied in making a living. The war in Vietnam, is easily explained as the fault of the communists and American interference. Intellectuals, on the other hand, are becoming more and more anti-American as the war continues in Vietnam. They point to the crises and shortages in the country, the poverty of the farmers, the bad roads, while the government has already given nearly $10 million to maintain army units in Vietnam. Social grievances are being linked with American policy in Southeast Asia and United States' investments in the Philippines.

In the midst of all this social and economic upheaval the Christian Filipino, unlike the Chinese minority which remains loyal to its cultural heritage, is desperately trying the establish his identity as an Asian in a region where his Muslim and Buddhist neighbours consider him to be simply an American in disguise. The two main features of Filipino society are still Western oriented, the first being Christianity and culture from Spain, the second, American concepts of democracy and free enterprise. Though the Filipinos may claim to be Asian at heart, they differ from other Orientals in many ways. Yet despite the social and technological changes which are taking place, notably in the urban areas, which are influenced by Western economic and political dominance, the Philippines are by no means westernized. This has resulted in the present dualism in outlook and a longing for a national identity. The consequences will certainly continue to influence Filipino perspectives within the foreseeable future.

8   Government, politics and education

THE PHILIPPINES was one of the first of the new Asian nations to achieve independence after the Second World War. Its Constitution patterned after that of the United States, provides for the separation of powers between the executive and the legislature. The vote is given to all male and female citizens, over twenty-one who are literate. This provision of literacy disenfranchises many of the poor and the tribal minorities; and in practice it deprives nearly half of the adult population of a chance to express its views at the polls.

Executive power is vested in the president who is elected for a term of four years and may be re-elected. With the approval of the Commission on Appointments of Congress, the president appoints the heads of governmental departments such as justice, foreign affairs, finance, health, education, national defence, public works and communications, labour, welfare, commerce and industry, and agriculture and natural resources. Among many other offices responsible to the chief executive are the Bureau of Civil Service, the Budget Commission, the National Economic Council and the Central Bank which is charged with administering the monetary and banking system of the Republic.

As commander-in-chief of the armed forces, the president is able to prevent or suppress insurrections, lawlessness and invasion and, if necessary, to place any part of the archipelago under martial law. He has greater unchecked powers than the United States' president does and can suspend provincial governors and mayors, grant pardons and commute sentences for all offences except in cases of impeachment. Treaties may be concluded with foreign

118

countries, subject to senate approval. In addition, the president, with the consent of the Commission on Appointments, appoints ambassadors and other diplomatic officials.

The vice-president is similarly elected for a term of four years and has a more or less ceremonial role, although in the event of the president's death, he assumes the presidential powers during the unexpired term of office. When he belongs to the same political party as the president, he usually obtains a cabinet portfolio.

Legislative power is vested in a bicameral congress composed of an upper house or senate, with twenty-four members elected by general suffrage for six-year terms, with one-third of the seats being contested every two years. The term of office for each senator begins on 30 December following his election. The House of Representatives, or lower house, has 120 seats apportioned among the different provinces according to population. However, the constitution provides that each province, irrespective of population, shall have at least one representative. A representative serves for a term of four years and, like a senator, is eligible for re-election.

The Congress normally convenes in regular session on the fourth Monday of January, but may be called by the president to a special session to consider urgent legislation. Regular sessions are limited to one hundred days, exclusive of Sundays. The two houses elect their own officers. As in the United States, the chief officer of the upper house is the President of the Senate, and in the lower house, the Speaker. Twelve members from each house constitute the Commission on Appointments of Congress. Congress has the sole power to make or amend laws, although a bill passed by the congress cannot become law unless the president signs it. A bill vetoed by him becomes law only if passed for a second time by a two-thirds majority of all the members of the two houses. In a national emergency only congress has the power to declare war and authorize the president to issue executive orders in furtherance of national policy.

The power of the judiciary is vested in the supreme court and in minor courts established by law. The supreme court consists of a chief justice and ten associates who rule upon the constitutionality of many legislative and executive acts, thus providing a check against illegal executive orders and regulations. Judges of the supreme court are appointed by the president with the consent of the commission on appointments. The court is also the presidential Electoral Tribunal. In addition, three judges of the court serve on each of the Senate and House of Representatives Electoral Tribunals.

Below the supreme court are a court of appeal, courts of agrarian and industrial relations, courts of first instance, municipal courts of chartered cities and justices of the peace. Unlike the American system, a jury is not used and cases are heard by justices. The appointment of the justices of the various courts is the responsibility of Congress, although it cannot deprive the supreme court of its ultimate jurisdiction over cases submitted from a lower court.

The legal profession is well established in the Philippines and, as in many countries, it has a special appeal to enterprising young men who see it as a stepping stone to political office. Civil and political liberties are jealously guarded, the press and radio being assured of freedom from governmental directives.

Notwithstanding the introduction of a Republican style of government, the centralization characteristic of the Spanish era still survives. Although there is a certain amount of autonomy in local government it is subject in the last resort to the ruling of the president in matters of finance and policy. This has, in many cases, led to over-centralization and undue dependence on the central government. The country is, at present, divided into fifty-six provinces, each consisting of cities and municipalities. Every province has its own governor heading a provincial board with two other members. This board is the legislative organ of the provincial government. The provincial governor and the other two members of the board serve for a term of four years, but have limited authority, as the central government makes appointments to the offices of provincial treasurer, fiscal and chief legal officer, as well as judge of the court of first instance, district health officer, district engineer, etc.—all serving under their respective departments of the central administration. The governor exercises general supervisory powers over the province and makes sure that all laws and regulations of the administration are known and carried out. Provinces are classified according to their income from rates and taxes and attain the designation of First Class A when the amount exceeds 500,000 pesos, graduating to Fifth Class when the income is less than 50,000 pesos. A few provinces are governed by special laws in view of the different culture of the tribal minorities.

Each municipality is a public corporation formed by an act of Congress and governed by the Municipal Law which defines its powers and duties, it consists of a town centre, often called *poblacion*, and a surrounding area separated into village units called barrios. Municipal officials appointed by the central government include the treasurer, the justice of the peace and the chief of police. Those elected (for terms of four years) are the mayor, vice-mayor, councillors and assistants known as lieutenants or *teniente del barrio* who are normally responsible to individual councillors for the maintenance of law and order in the respective barrios. Local government is carried on from the municipal hall, still known as the *presidencia*.[47]

Like the province, the municipality has limited fiscal powers. This has meant a dependence upon the allocation of funds by the central government which, in turn, is subject to the influence of local businessmen and large landowners. However measures have been taken since independence to check this unhealthy tendency to over-centralization and to allow local administrations fuller use of their powers and privileges, especially in the case of the chartered cities, which have been created by a special act of congress. This act, which also serves as the city charter, can only be repealed or amended by congress. At present there are thirty-nine chartered cities, including Manila and the official capital, Quezon City. Each city council levies and collects taxes in accordance with the law and makes by-laws. In addition, it maintains a local police force and is responsible for public works.

The day-to-day working of the national administrative machine is influenced at every level by politics and the privileged status of members of Congress, who are able to extend patronage to their supporters as well as to members of their own family circle. The full extent of this paternalistic role is revealed when congressmen debate and enact every year the bill allocating funds to the communities for public and social improvements. This is known popularly as the 'pork barrel bill'; each senator and congressman allocating a sum of money for public improvements, which he often does with the object of maintaining political influence and local popularity. In return the politician is besieged by many who seek redress for grievances and employment, usually in government departments. The perpetuation of this practice has led to a serious undermining of the independence and impartiality of the civil service.[48]

Although Filipino politics show all the signs of American influence it has, nevertheless, an intensely personal character. The key to an understanding of the political system is the concept of the pre-Spanish Datu, who not only ruled his people but adopted the role of father figure, settled disputes and rewarded his followers for good service. The twentieth-century Filipino is no exception. He still prefers strong individual leadership which dispenses favours and offers the possibility of protection. In the Philippines the supreme leader who can fill this role is the president. All classes of the people will go to him, if at all possible, to air their grievances and make requests, rather than to the appropriate government department. This was a fundamental reason for the strong respect and popularity of Magsaysay. He not only went to the people but encouraged them to visit his official residence, Malacanang. This policy was repeated by Macapagal, who in many cases dealt with petitions on the spot.

This system of patronage is not confined to the president; it repeats itself on a lesser scale at every level of political leadership. A patron soon has a following which may be distributed over the whole archipelago. In general it is true to say that the basic structure of the two or three political parties is made up of a leader or leaders who bring their respective supporters with them.

As discussed earlier, party loyalty is usually one of convenience and depends largely on which way the political wind is blowing. Whatever course is taken, personal supporters follow likewise, as they owe allegiance to the leader and not to the party. Consequently, the importance of the supporting group is mostly felt at the polls.

According to the Election Code, a candidate for congress must not spend more on electioneering than one year's official salary. He is prohibited from buying votes, providing gifts, free food and drink. At election time all this is conveniently forgotten and candidates spend large amounts to further their campaign. One who is not rich or financed by wealthy interests has little chance of entering congress. The majority of elected members have a living standard which far exceeds that possible on their official salary. In short, political survival in the Philippines at the present time requires that one must be wealthy, have strong financial backing, be in with the winning party and in general have the same social ideology.

The domination of the political structure by the caciques and powerful vested interests, both foreign and Filipino, will no doubt continue until the bulk of the electorate has developed into a more national body representing all classes and interests, not least the cultural minorities. The most important factor in developing a political awareness is education. Despite the fact, however, that today practically every part of the archipelago has a school of sorts, the present quality of the teaching leaves much to be desired. In many cases it is totally inadequate, with a frightening shortage of textbooks and essential materials. Another significant feature of the present educational system is the widespread influence of the private schools, and their development as money-making institutions, with little regard for the quality of schooling or the value of a diploma issued to an unsuspecting pupil.

Historically, what is called modern education in the Philippines dates from the early years of the Spanish colonizers and the introduction of the Catholic faith. It consisted mainly of teaching the essentials of Christianity, arithmetic, reading and writing through the use of native dialects. Later on the friars and Spanish authorities provided limited opportunities for higher education, including instruction in Spanish, but this was only available to a few. It was not until the American occupation that mass education was introduced to wipe out widespread illiteracy. The introduction of English eventually assisted in unifying the people of the different regions, and became a means of communication among the many linguistic groups as the public school system under the American régime developed and expanded. During the Commonwealth period the public educational system had to readjust itself in view of the educational aims embodied in the draft constitution. Aims included the need to develop moral character, personal discipline, civic conscience, vocational efficiency and the appreciation of citizenship. Attention was drawn to the use of Tagalog—now called Pilipino—as the basis for a national language and as a subject to be taught in all schools. The aim of the government was to provide, at least, free education at a primary school level.

During the Commonwealth era the National Council of Education was created to study the educational needs and problems facing the country. Moves were made to reduce adult illiteracy and supervise the operation of private schools and colleges. In 1940 President Quezon approved the Commonwealth Act No. 570, which declared a modified form of Tagalog as one of the three official languages, the other two being English and Spanish. The outbreak of the Second World War and the Japanese occupation brought to a halt the considerable expansion of the educational system which had been achieved during the years 1935-41, when the number of public schools increased from some 7,000 to more than 12,000. The schools were reorganized by the Japanese to eliminate all traces of American influence from the curriculum. Although English was retained as a language of instruction, Tagalog and Japanese were stressed and given priority.

The inevitable outcome of war resulted in considerable damage to school buildings and the destruction of books and materials. After the liberation and the establishment of the Republic, active steps were taken to resuscitate the school system. Education became one of the largest items in the budget, and growing emphasis was placed upon functional instruction in the rural areas, the provision of community schools in the barrios, and a new concept of the teacher's role. This was to guide and assist both adult and child in subjects such as agriculture, sanitation, health, homes and communities. By 1956 the number of public schools had increased to 25,000, with a total enrolment of 3,500,000 and nearly 100,000 teachers. Private schools numbered more than 2,000 and had an estimated enrolment of nearly a million. Already the Board of National Education, the highest educational policy-making authority, had completed the preparation of a programme evolving a new system to meet the new status of the Philippines. Changes were made to improve the standards of instruction in the schools. These were the adoption of national examinations for fourth-year secondary school and college students, as well as fourth-form primary school pupils. In 1957 the teaching of Spanish was made obligatory in all secondary schools. This was a victory for the small but influential pro-Spanish element in the Philippines which had been waging an unremitting campaign for the revival of the language as the first step towards closer contact with Latin America.

Many revisions affecting the private schools, such as the adoption and implementation of national examinations at the fourth-year level, met with a storm of protests from various bodies including the Catholic Educational Association of the Philippines. The objectors claimed that the examinations were unconstitutional, that the government wanted to take over the control of curricula and the choice of text-books. Such protests from those with investments and financial interests in the numerous schools, colleges and universities were not unexpected. The Filipino passion for prestige and a diploma as a status symbol had created a lucrative source of income for many private schools not financially assisted by the government. While keeping their financial investment per student as low as possible, schools admit as many students as possible without any rigorous conditions for entry. Unfortunately, the popular clamour for education in name has assisted many vested interests in thwarting the efforts of those within and without the government to impose educational standards in private schools. This is one of the fundamental reasons why, despite large enrolments, the quality of education is generally low. Nowhere is this more obvious than in the colleges and universities where the tuition, facilities and equipment are often inadequate to meet even the lowest academic standards, especially when compared to the state-run University of the Philippines.[49]

The whole question of improving educational standards in the

Philippines is one which can only be solved by the government. Unfortunately, its efforts have hitherto been hampered by legalities and politics. At the moment about one-third of the national budget is spent on education, mainly in an endeavour to comply with the constitutional requirement that free schooling shall be provided for all at the primary school level. By 1962 the number of primary schools increased to nearly 32,000, as compared to about 1,800 secondary schools and some 400 colleges, including universities of various kinds. The public schools comprised more than 90 per cent of all primary schools in the archipelago, but only a mere 23 per cent of secondary schools and between 12 and 14 per cent of colleges and universities. The distribution of enrolment between the public and private schools followed the same general pattern, most of the secondary and college students being absorbed in the private institutions.

While the government can point to the large increase in the number of primary schools as a visible political accomplishment, little has been done, either directly or with the assistance of foreign aid, to provide the necessary text-books and equipment urgently needed to prevent further deterioration in the quality of the public schools. Coupled with the controversy over a national language, the use of native dialect in the home and poor teaching methods have resulted in a marked decline in the standard of English reached in the schools. Although the public schools account for the large majority at the primary level, it is significant that only about half of the children complete the first four years. Barely one-third complete the sixth year and move on to higher education. For economic reasons about 10 per cent of the children of school age are unable to attend school. Unless agrarian reform and other measures are taken to improve the general standard of living for the majority of people, especially in the rural areas, an increase in non-attendance at the primary level will result.

The United States has given aid to Philippine education, and between 1951 and 1962 spent approximately $20,000,000 on education and vocational training. Additional aid has come from the Colombo Plan, United Nations Technical Assistance and other foreign sources. Because of the lack of local funds and non-implementation of projects, the overall result, allowing for a number of achievements, has been disappointing to many Filipinos. Every year the Department of Education has to haggle for money to meet teachers' salaries and this, of course, causes a lowering of morale among the teachers. Although President Marcos emphasized in May 1966 that the future of the country lies in the hands of the young, little has been done by his administration to rectify the problems of educating Filipinos.

19 A modern school and Ifugao village near Banaue, Mt. Province.

20 The main building of the University of Sto. Thomas, Manila, founded in the 17th century by Dominican friars.

21 These dancers are doing the Tinikling, one of the best-known of Philippine dances. The man is wearing a Barong Tagalog and the woman, a form of Balintawak.

22 Muslim girls perform a slow-moving and elegant folk-dance.

23 A 'Musikong Bumbong' or bamboo band, taking part in a procession.

24 The Ifugaos are talented and artistic woodcarvers. The carving at left is probably of the artist's head-hunter ancestor.

25 In the country districts, the potter's wheel is still in use for making pots and jars.

26 Above left: although modern methods of lumbering are employed, a large part of the work is still performed manually.

27 An Ifugaoan peasant (far left) leaving his tobacco field.

28 Coconut growing (left) provides a livelihood for thousands of small farmers.

29 Above: with the aid of the carabao, heavy presses squeeze the rich juice from sugar cane. Primitive as the arrangement is, it is useful in the remote regions of the archipelago, where there are no sugar refineries.

30 An Ifugaoan weaver at a vocational school in the Mt. Province (right).

31 A tropical fruit stall on the main road outside Manila.

32 The export of canned pineapple is a growing industry but not yet a major one for the Philippines.

33 Fishing rafts built primarily of bamboo, are used extensively in coves and the mouths of rivers. Nets hang from the long boom anchored on a pivot to the deck.

34 These rice terraces near Banaue, Mt. Province, were carved out of the mountain slopes by the Ifugaos more than 2000 years ago.

35 Buses are the main form of long-distance transport for the ordinary Filipino. At many stops, vendors sell refreshments through the bus windows.

36 Cock fights are a vital part of Filipino life, where family fortunes are often won and lost.

9   The economy

Although the Philippine economy has undergone a number of far-reaching changes, both before and after independence, it is still largely agricultural with the bulk of the population living in the rural areas. The importance of agriculture has, to an extent, concealed the vast potential of the islands with their great unexploited deposits of minerals, forests, fisheries, and possibilities for hydroelectric power.

As already stated, the inhabitants of the Philippine archipelago were trading with China, Japan and other parts of the Orient long before the Spaniards took possession in 1565. The trans-Pacific galleon trade which developed between the Philippines and Mexico involved the transportation of selected crops, sugar being the first commodity to be exported by the Spaniards. During the eighteenth century the growth of sugar production was slow and inefficient until modern machinery was introduced in the Visayas during the middle part of the nineteenth century by Nicholas Loney, a British merchant in Iloilo. Within a few years sugar mills operated by steam were in action in Negros, where a rich soil and a favourable climate combined to make the region the most productive in the Philippines. At first the yearly output was about 12,000 tons and increased until the turn of the century, when it rose sharply as a result of the American market and the stimulation of free trade, reaching a record of 1,598,000 short tons in 1933. A setback occurred when American and Cuban interests, fearing competition from the Philippines, persuaded the United States Congress to introduce a quota system regulating sugar imports. This was followed in May 1934 by the Jones-Costigan Bill, when the Philippine quota was

L

fixed at 850,000 tons. Eventually however, production recovered; and at the outbreak of the Second World War reached the one-million-ton level.

During the war and the Japanese occupation, serious damage was caused to the mills and plantations. It was not until 1953 that the sugar industry was able to fulfil the new United States quota of 980,000 tons and meet increases in domestic consumption as well. Since then, expansion has been influenced by small increases in local consumption, the dispute between the United States and Cuba and the withdrawal of Cuban sugar from the world market in 1962. The United States Sugar Act, which assigned Cuba's former global quota, 16 per cent of the market, meant an increase of nearly 50 per cent in the Philippine quota. While this gave certain encouragement and impetus to the numerous small sugar planters in the archipelago, who in general do not own more than 20 to 30 acres of land and constitute the backbone of the industry, it was recognized that the Cuban crisis might not last for an indefinite period. Already the cost of producing and handling Philippine sugar was too high to be competitive in world markets. A profit has been made only because of the premium price paid in the American market.

When the Laurel-Langley Agreement is terminated in 1974, the Philippines will lose her privileged quota position. This could cause disaster to the industry if other markets are not found. Efforts must be made to increase efficiency by extensive mechanization and centralization and by the promotion and sale of various by-products of sugar. Whether the government will negotiate with the United States for an extension of the Laurel-Langley Agreement is not certain. An extension might solve the problem of maintaining a guaranteed quota and reduce the risk of agrarian unrest. In the long term an extension could only result in a perpetuation of American influence over the economy. Although sugar exports, solely to the United States, increased by 5 per cent in 1965, production decreased to some 1,432,000 short tons, a fall about 8 per cent. During the first half of 1966 sugar exports declined by 3 per cent from the corresponding period in 1965, influenced by a reduction in output and increased home consumption. Accordingly, the Philippines

138

decided to give up 100,000 short tons of its extra sugar quota in the American market in 1966. This was followed, however, by a government decision to import sugar from Thailand in 1967 to meet increased domestic consumption and the quota to be exported to United States. In 1966, because of a sugar shortage in the United States, the Philippines had been allowed 195,693 tons in addition to its quota of 1,061,000 short tons. However, it could not fill more than 49 per cent of this extra share. The sugar export price has moved upward since the beginning of 1966 because of the support given by the United States market price; and this clearly illustrates the benefit of the Laurel-Langley Agreement. The price was $6·22 per 100 lb. in December 1966 as against $1·95 per 100 lb. for Taiwan sugar the same year.

As in Indonesia and other parts of Southeast Asia, the coconut palm has been the chief food-producing tree; and being a native tropical palm it is not surprising that the coconut trade is one of the oldest in the Philippines, dating back to pre-Spanish times. Not only is the coconut the most valuable and versatile agricultural crop, supplying basic food, clothing and shelter for people on the islands, but it is also the most important export product of the archipelago, with its by-products, copra, desiccated coconut, copra meal and coconut oil. After the United States occupation coconut growing became a dominant factor of the Philippine economy and in 1959 accounted for nearly 30 per cent of the total exports as against 24 per cent in 1939.

Coconut palms are widely distributed throughout the islands and grow chiefly in the coastal districts, with a few regions specializing in commercial production. The most important are the areas southeast of Manila and parts of eastern and southern Luzon. Other regions of importance are found in the Visayas and Mindanao. Coconuts are traditionally considered the lazy man's crop: a ripe nut falls, germinates, sinks its roots in the soil and in a few years the seedling becomes a tree and nuts fall again. Today many of the seed nuts are planted in nurseries and are transplanted during the rainy season when the shoots are about nine months old. Fruit bearing starts about seven years later. Fruit-bearing trees in the

Philippines were estimated at 150 million in 1963 and increase at a rate of about 3 million trees annually. A harvest of some 7,000 million nuts makes the Philippines the world's leading supplier of coconuts and coconut products, especially dried coconut meat or copra which, together with coconut oil, is much in demand in the United States and Europe for making soap, lotions and perfumes as well as for cooking purposes. Coconut oil is often stockpiled, as it is used extensively in the manufacture of synthetic-rubber plasticizers, resins, sulfonated alcohols, glycerine, dyes, and many other items.

Whether the Philippines will be able to maintain its present position in world production is still uncertain. Indonesia and Thailand have developed their coconut growing, and steps have been taken to increase production in India and some African countries. As in the case of sugar, the Laurel-Langley Agreement is important when assessing future trends in the foreign markets, with the problems of restrictions on imports of coconut oil into the United States, and in Europe into the member countries of the European Common Market. While copra is imported into the United States free of duty, coconut oil is subject to a diminishing duty-free quota which amounted to 80,000 long tons in 1968, and will decrease to 40,000 in 1971 and nil in 1974.

The creation in 1954 of the Philippine Coconut Administration as a co-ordinating element for the industry paved the way for the formation in 1963 of the United Philippine Coconut Association (UPCA) to represent the different interests and deal with a number of problems. This organization provided a united front for presenting bills in congress and in dealing with foreign and domestic problems of marketing, productivity, the control of pests and diseases and the elimination of the deadly cadang cadang disease, etc. The Association encourages new plantings of coconut seedlings. However, concern has been expressed over the estimated expansion of coconut plantings, which average about 100,000 new acres every year, and whether increased productivity can be absorbed by domestic consumption. According to an ECAFE report of 1966–67, the Philippines produced about 43 per cent of the world's coconut

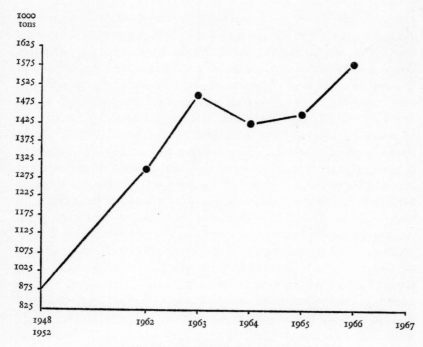

1000
tons

Fig 1 Production of Copra between 1952-66

products and exported about 65 per cent of these. See Fig. 1. Cost of production is high and must be reduced if the industry is to be competitive. Export earnings from copra and coconut products total roughly $250,000,000 annually and provide, directly or indirectly, a living for approximately one out of every four Filipinos.

Abacá fibre, one of the most valuable of all fibres for cordage, is the product of *Musa textilis*, a plant of the banana family, commercially known as Manila hemp. Some Central American countries and India have tried to cultivate the plant, but with only limited success. Abacá thrives best in a rich and moist soil and requires rain throughout the year, conditions found in the eastern parts of the Philippines.

The abacá plant is concentrated in southeast Luzon, eastern Visayas and southeast Mindanao. During the early part of the present century in the Davao region of Mindanao a rapid expansion of abacá cultivation was stimulated by Japanese settlers. After the Second World War, Japanese plantations were confiscated and distributed among Filipino smallholders who replaced much of the abacá with food crops. Since then attempts to restore abacá growing to pre-war levels have not succeeded. From a production of 48,000 long tons, in 1946 the best level was reached with 98,000 long tons in 1955, decreasing again to 95,000 longs tons in 1960. At the moment it is a declining industry faced with a number of problems, including plant disease and competition from metallic and synthetic fibres. In 1962 the Macapagal administration launched a five-year abacá development programme designed to raise production to a level equal to the predicted figure of world consumption. The outcome of this programme is uncertain, though exports of abacá in 1964 were about 10 per cent higher than those in the previous year. In 1965 exports decreased, and the production of abacá fibre decreased to 107,800 tons, a backward trend towards the production level of 1962. The decline continued through 1966, and in 1967 output had fallen to 86,000 tons.

Other crops of importance are pineapples and tobacco. Pineapples are grown throughout the archipelago, and are eaten as a household fruit; a large export industry has developed as a result of American investment, principally in northern Mindanao, where commercial growing and canning in modern factories has shown a steady increase. The f.o.b. value of canned pineapple now exceeds $12 million annually. The Philippines is the fourth largest producer of canned pineapple, superseded only by the United States, Taiwan and Malaysia. A new project financed by a Honolulu company is expected to increase the export of canned pineapples to $40 million in 1970. Though tobacco growing is the eighth largest agricultural crop, it outranks any other in its contribution to the national exchequer and as a means of employment—directly of indirectly—for some four million Filipinos.

Tobacco and its by-products have produced revenue since 1782, when a monopoly was established by the Spanish authorities. The monopoly was abolished in 1882, and private capital was invested in large plantations and improved facilities for manufacturing. Today the industry is divided into two parts, the first producing the Virginia or aromatic type of cigarette tobacco, and the second the native tobacco used in the manufacture of cigars and black cigarettes. The industry suffered considerably from the effects of the Second World War and the loss of the American and other foreign markets. When trading was resumed, production was barely 50 per cent of the pre-war level and continued at this level until the dispute between the United States and Cuba forced American tobacco interests to look once more towards the Philippines. In 1953 the United States imported nearly three million Manila cigars, a mere 17 per cent of the total imports compared with Cuba's 80 per cent. In 1962 imports from the Philippines reached 13·3 million cigars or 85 per cent of the total as a result of the American embargo on Cuban tobacco. By 1967 more than 200,000 acres of Philippine land were used for tobacco growing. Through the Philippine Tobacco Administration, the industry enjoys price supports and this has benefited growers in the Cagayan Valley, which is the most important native tobacco-producing region in the Philippines. The industry has yet to attain the position it once held before the Second World War, being faced with a number of problems common to other industries in the Philippines, such as the need to expand its exports, reduce production costs, find new markets and improve its quotas under the Laurel-Langley Agreement.

In 1965, two proposals aimed at stabilizing the growing and marketing of Virginia tobacco were put forward by the Philippine Virginia Tobacco Administration and the Secretary of Commerce in Macapagal's administration. The first proposal recommended the gradual withdrawal of the government price subsidy so that locally grown Virginia leaf tobacco could find its own price level. The second proposal recommended government assistance to stimulate exports, instead of government stockpiling which discouraged exports. It was reported that the Philippine Virginia Tobacco Administration had tobacco stocks dating back as far as the 1961 crop, with a value of almost $70 million. At the same time the smuggling and sale of cigarettes openly, known as blue seal, has grown into a large and lucrative business. By 1966 smuggling had become a serious problem for the tobacco industry. Many factories had been forced to run at only 50 per cent of their capacity and the industry itself was faced with a restrictive credit policy by the government. As yet, the 1965 proposals have not been implemented.

Among food crops grown for domestic consumption, rice is the most important and, at the same time, the problem child of the economy. Though the Philippines has enough land, the proper climate and more than enough people to produce rice, the country is plagued every year with shortages, a result of yields which are the lowest in Southeast Asia. From 1900 up to a year ago, rice had been imported every year except in a year or two before the Second World War and in 1953, 1959 and 1960, when reserves met the domestic requirements. While the farmer is blamed for the low yields because of his primitive farming methods, two primary causes would seem to be the limited development of wet-rice cultivation in pre-Spanish times and the later adoption in certain areas of corn as the principal food grain. Corn, rather than dry-rice, is often planted by those who rotate their crops, and in many areas, especially in the Visayas, corn planting has caused severe soil erosion. Corn is cheaper to grow than rice and is the main item in the diet of about 25 per cent of the population.

There are a number of other factors affecting the recurring rice shortages, such as poor incentives to rice farmers, ineffective credit facilities, the archaic land tenure system, the unrealistic price of rice grain (*palay*), the poor quality of seeds, lack of irrigation and proper fertilization, etc. While these factors certainly contribute to the shortages, there are other reasons, such as inadequate storage facilities, the low government price supports. Theoretically, the Rice Tenancy Act should assure the rice growing tenant 70 per cent return from the harvest when he uses his own implements, animals and seed. In practice the law is seldom observed and the majority of tenants, who earn less than $500 a year, are unable to buy fertilizers or essential equipment without going into debt to middlemen and absentee lords who charge high rates of interest.

The International Rice Research Institute at Los Banos, supported by the Rockefeller and Ford Foundations, has attempted to solve the problems affecting rice production and the discovery and propagation of IR-8 or 'miracle rice' has increased the 1967-68 harvest. On an experimental farm 8½ tons of IR-8 rice were grown from one acre of land in 12 months, about 15 times the average yield in the tropics.[50]

Though miracle rice may help to cut imports, the fundamental causes affecting productivity, such as the farmers' lack of incentive, remain. In 1963 President Macapagal introduced legislation to eradicate the share tenancy system and substitute a new leasehold and land-ownership system; but the opposition to these proposals insisted on considerable modifications to his original concept. The final form and implementation of the legislation is still an open question and represents in 1968 a challenge to President Marcos, who has hitherto only paid lip service to the reform.[51]

Despite a large increase in overall food production since the Second World War, the archipelago has become more dependent than ever on imports to offset shortages of meat and dairy products. Imported food also helps to counter malnutrition, caused largely by the starchy diet based on rice and corn, supplemented with roots, vegetables, meat and fish only when the household economy permits.[52] Domestic shortages and the cost of importing foodstuffs in 1966 caused food prices to rise faster than the cost of living. The future of the livestock industry in the Philippines is uncertain, and hitherto the government has done little to assist the farmer to improve his methods of breeding and feeding. The present rate of slaughter is far too high, and if allowed to continue will decimate the cattle population within a number of years. The absurdity of the situation is that the Philippines has extensive grasslands, its climate is suitable for growing pasture throughout the year, and watering is no problem. Yet with all the favourable circumstances for raising livestock the industry remains in its infancy. Meat is imported, and the average Filipino eats only approximately 30–35 lb. of meat per

M

year compared with 250 lb. *per capita* consumption in Australia and New Zealand.[53]

Milk production, suffers from the same problems, and Philippine cows supply only about 5 per cent of the total milk consumption.

	Production of Dairy Products in thousand tons*					
	1948 1952	1962	1963	1964	1965	1966
Cow	1	1	1	1	—	—
Buffalo	1	6	6	6	—	—

*Source: FAO.

Rice supplemented with fish is a common meal for the majority of Filipinos. Despite the fact that the Philippines has one of the richest and most extensive fishing grounds in the world, the country is obliged to import fish every year. Potential fishery resources consist of about 2 million acres of fresh water and some 400 million acres of marine areas. Here, as related earlier, are to be found more than 2,000 species of fish, ranging in size from the giant shark to the tiny goby. The productivity of large stretches of coastal waters is beginning to decline. This is because of the irresponsible and prevalent method of dynamite fishing, concentrated in rivers and relatively shallow water not exceeding 150 feet. There is a general reluctance to engage in deep-sea fishing without government guarantees and capital to purchase fishing boats and equipment. In addition, the lack of cold storage and organized distribution usually results in seasonal gluts accompanied by low prices. Although Filipinos have shown great skill in developing the raising of fish in ponds by means of artificial fertilization, the average yield is one of the lowest in the world, being about one-fifth of a ton per acre compared to Formosa, which averages nearly one ton per acre.

In 1963 the Philippine Congress approved a bill creating a fisheries commission to help develop the fishing industry. The

United Nations Special Fund also has a large-scale project in the Philippines to improve fishing at a cost of $3,745,150 over five years. In February 1968 a fishery and research training vessel left England for Manila to take part in deep-sea development projects. These projects, together with one aimed at intensifying agricultural training in Mindanao, should make an important contribution to the economy.

During 1965 the fish catch totalled 667,202 metric tons but was still far short of the national demand, estimated by the government as 991,698 metric tons. The basis for this figure is the dietary requirement to maintain a *per capita* consumption of about 65 pounds. Towards the middle of 1964 Macapagal announced the implementation of a three-year fish production programme, calculated to double production in at least thirty-eight provinces. However, there was not sufficient money to make this programme effective. Imports of fish and fish products are still running at a high level and will continue to do so unless drastic measures are taken quickly by President Marcos and his administration to put the industry on a sound footing.

The exploitation of the extensive stands of tropical hardwoods has brought the lumber industry to third place in the country's exports. Much of the output is the result of a number of logging companies working on the short-term policy of obtaining a quick profit and then moving on, a policy which presents a threat to the future of timber and water resources in the archipelago. Already in many parts denuded slopes and clearings show signs of soil erosion, indicating the need for strong government policy and scientific management. If cutting were properly controlled, according to conservation practices, the lumber industry has the potential of being one of the most important factors in the national economy. Apart from providing employment for an estimated 170,000 Filipinos, the industry also supplies a considerable amount of material used in building construction and has the opportunity of contributing by-products to the cottage industries, especially furniture making. Of the total land area of the Philippines more than twenty-three million acres are covered with commercial forests, the present volume of standing timber being assessed at 408,000 million board feet. By the end of 1965, more than twenty factories turning out plywood and ten factories making veneers were in operation, a significant increase from the three plants for making plywood operating in the 1950s. Plans have been made for the first fully integrated pulp and paper-mill. There are many possibilities open to the industry if various problems can be solved in the near future, e.g. the formulation of a national lumber policy, the control of concessions, availability of financial credits, building of better facilities for transporting lumber from the forests to specified centres, communications, the training of labour, reduction of freight charges, improved marketing and the exploitation of less important timber trees and waste products including forest plants. Timber stands were steadily diminishing in 1967 due to illegal cutting and the practice of caingin or shifting cultivation.

The mineral wealth of the Philippines includes deposits of gold, silver, iron, lead, zinc, copper, manganese and chrome. The chrome deposit covers more than 1,000 acres in the province of Zambales, and is believed to be one of the largest in the world. Large parts of the islands have never been explored or made the subject of a geological survey, and the real wealth of the archipelago is largely unknown although, there are indications of deposits of natural gas, phosphates, sulphur and low and medium-grade coal.

The mining of gold and iron in a primitive fashion dates back to pre-Spanish times, while coal-mining is believed to have started sometime during the early part of the nineteenth century. With the arrival of American prospectors after 1900, many of them discharged servicemen, gold mining was expanded by the use of modern methods and a number of former gold and silver mines were brought into production again, especially in the Mountain Province where output was enhanced by the boom of 1932–36. During the Second World War and the Japanese occupation many of the mines were devastated. After liberation the industry as a whole was the last to be rehabilitated. Both gold and silver mining have declined owing to increasing costs of production and more or less fixed market prices, with the result that while gold and silver are

148

still exported there has been a noticeable shift to the mining of copper, chromite and iron ore. Between 1968 and 1969 at least three new copper mines are expected to go into production. Production of manganese has declined slightly during the last few years, while mercury and molybdenum are produced in relatively small quantities. The output of other minerals such as cement, salt, sand and gravel has shown an increase since 1960.

In the past, smelting and refining have been done outside the Philippines. Now copper smelting and the processing of other metals will become a local activity, although the almost complete absence of coal and home-produced oil are serious drawbacks to development, The expansion of smelting depends greatly on the availability of hydro-electric power. A most significant development is the multi-purpose Angat project to boost the power supply for Luzon and Manila. Unfortunately, power from the National Power Corporation is not available everywhere in the archipelago, and the large number of private power franchises in provincial districts, with their high tariffs, sometimes exorbitant, have acted as a deterrent to schemes for modernizing the towns and barrios.

Since the creation of the Commonwealth, a number of light industries have been set up by government initiative. These now produce shoes, minor rubber products, canned foods, clothing, textiles, dyes, glass, and pharmaceutical products including antibiotics and vitamins. Recently the textile industry, which was originally started by the government and then handed over to private enterprise, has shown signs of collapsing, despite its increasing production. By 1965 only five textile manufacturing companies out of twenty-four were in operation, and unemployment was on the increase. One of the main reasons for the shutting down of these factories has been the competition of smuggled goods. However, the government's drive to curb widespread smuggling—which has the support of many influential people in business and politics—has had some success and after a difficult period in 1966-67 the industry has begun to recover.

The oil industry is important to the economy and supplies nearly 95 per cent of the country's fuel; its by-products include liquefied

149

petroleum, petrol, paraffin, bunker and diesel oil and asphalt. The monthly production is estimated to be 500,000 tons at the present time and national consumption of all petroleum products indicates an average annual increase of 7.5 per cent. The industry is a large employer of local labour, and has a capital investment of $150 million. To keep the local refineries in operation it is necessary to import some $90 million worth of crude oil every year. This has spurred efforts to determine whether the Philippines has substantial oil reserves. Hitherto, more than 25 million acres have been surveyed, but no significant deposits have yet been discovered. In 1963 the first Filipino-owned and operated refinery, called Filoil, started while foreign oil companies began to expand more into petro-chemical fields with plans to build nitrogenous fertilizer plants, and to market pesticides and insecticides.

Cement has been used in a small way for many years. The first cement factory was started in 1914 at Binangonan, in Rizal province. From then until after independence production has varied between 25,000 to 100,000 tons per year, excepting the war years. Between 1955–63 the output of cement doubled. Further increases are anticipated as a result of the projected construction of plants in Luzon and Mindanao coming into operation and supplementing the output from the existing ones in Luzon and in the Visayas. Until the cost of inter-island transportation is lowered, expansion will be retarded as costs begin to rise. The cement industry expected the 1968 output to rise to some 100 million bags.

The role of cottage industries in the Philippine economy has until recently received scant attention, although textiles made from Pina cloth, hand-woven from pineapple fibres and often embellished with fine hand embroidery, has been known abroad since Spanish days. Another well-known fabric is Jusi, usually made from raw-silk imported from China. This is used mostly for making women's clothing and it is also used (as is Pina) for making elegant embroidered shirts for men called the Barong Tagalog. Another fabric, much stronger than cotton, is Ramie, machine-woven from a flax-like plant grown in the Philippines and used to make trousers and shirts.

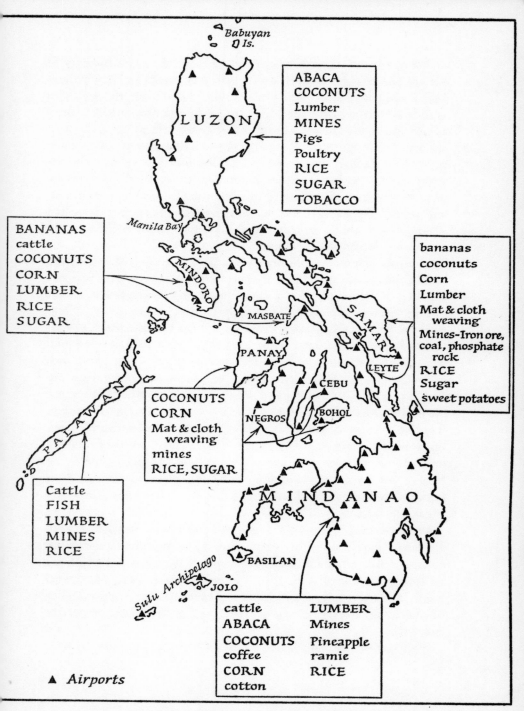

Babuyan Is.

LUZON

ABACA
COCONUTS
Lumber
MINES
Pigs
Poultry
RICE
SUGAR
TOBACCO

Manila Bay

BANANAS
cattle
COCONUTS
CORN
LUMBER
RICE
SUGAR

MINDORO

MASBATE

PANAY

SAMAR

LEYTE

bananas
coconuts
Corn
Lumber
Mat & cloth
weaving
Mines-Iron ore,
coal, phosphate
rock
RICE
Sugar
sweet potatoes

COCONUTS
CORN
Mat & cloth
weaving
mines
RICE, SUGAR

CEBU

NEGROS

BOHOL

PALAWAN

Cattle
FISH
LUMBER
MINES
RICE

MINDANAO

Sulu Archipelago

BASILAN

JOLO

cattle
ABACA
COCONUTS
coffee
CORN
cotton

LUMBER
Mines
Pineapple
ramie
RICE

▲ *Airports*

*Economic map of the Philippines. (Major crops and products
are shown in capital letters.)*

The thick iridescent mother-of-pearl from the giant bivalves of Cavite and Visayan waters are shaped into dinner plates, cigarette boxes and fancy jewellery, while Capiz shells from the southern islands are made into screens and lamps. In addition, intricate brass gongs and many other local products, contribute to the output of the handicraft industry. Realizing the potentialities of the cottage industries, Macapagal's administration established in 1962 a development authority (NACIDA) to encourage the growth of cottage industries by extending financial aid, granting certain tax exemptions and stimulating exports. In 1967 more than 20,705 cottage industries —employing about 56,000 workers—have been registered. In 1966 sales exceeded $1 million.

In organizing their economy the Filipinos have up to now adhered to the concept of limited government intervention and have adopted a policy of free enterprise, a choice reflecting the legacy from the United States. The years after independence were to an extent devoted to restoring, with American financial assistance, a war-ravaged economy. After a reduction of this aid in 1949, it was found necessary to impose import and exchange controls. This was followed in a few years by a policy of large-scale deficit financing and easy credit in an attempt to encourage business and reduce unemployment. The result was a succession of unbalanced budgets from 1953 to 1958, culminating in a deficit of approximately one-third of total expenditures. Such a fiscal and monetary policy opened the way to inflation and a renewal of the problem of balance of payments. Foreign exchange holdings dwindled as imports rapidly increased and resulted in the government imposing a maze of controls.

Between 1958 and 1961 the government made efforts to restore economic equilibrium by drastically curtailing public spending, raising certain taxes and imposing a special 25 per cent margin fee on foreign exchange sales. After he took office in 1962, Macapagal boldly terminated the programme and transferred the responsibility of allocating foreign exchange from the government to private enterprise.

President Macapagal's policy of de-control made definite changes in the economy. Claims were made that as a result export receipts had improved, imports had fallen and a reduction of the balance of payments deficit had been acomplished. In 1964, the government declared that de-control had been a success, but there was no doubt that the Philippines was in financial difficulty. In 1965 a $40 million load was granted by twelve American banks to help bolster agriculture and industry, while a Food for Peace agreement permitted the country to buy some 100,000 metric tons of rice from the United States for $12·5 million, payable in pesos, a move intended to support and conserve holdings of foreign exchange.

When Ferdinand Marcos succeeded to the presidency in 1966, the National Economic Council drafted a new socio-economic programme to implement the Land Reform Code formulated by the previous administration. The council also noted that the monetary and fiscal measures taken hitherto had not been adequate to achieve economic and social development. Problems considered to be hampering progress were the fact that national income for 1965, based on 1960 prices, had been 12,918 million pesos, and this amount, divided among a population of 32·3 million, meant a *per capita* income of 3,990 pesos, which is far too low. With production lagging behind population growth and unemployment increasing at a rate of 2 to 3 per cent, little imagination was needed to see the extent of poverty and low purchasing power. In 1968 nearly 25 per cent of the labour force was either unemployed or under-employed, while at the same time the administration was complaining about low agricultural productivity.

Rural areas have been badly neglected, many of which have a shortage of wells, roads, medical aid, communication facilities, electric power and household necessities, and some of them are inaccessible except by the most primitive means of travel. Income is unstable as the Philippines is primarily a supplier of raw materials and a consumer of articles manufactured and imported from other nations, while its free trade relations with the United States has made the archipelago dependent on American trade. In 1966 over 40 per cent of Philippine exports went to the United States, while less than 40 per cent of Philippine imports were supplied from

American sources. About 25 per cent of exports went to Japan and about the same percentage of imports came from there. The European Common Market countries occupied third place in the table of overseas trade, with West Germany the biggest consumer and supplier.[54] Talks were conducted in Washington concerning a renewal of the Laurel-Langley Agreement, probably in a revised form, so that parity rights would not be accorded to Americans while many of the existing preferential tariff features would be retained. In the Philippines there is a considerable American investment estimated at $600 million. There are about 800 American firms in the archipelago and some 400 owned jointly by U.S. and Philippine interests. These businesses are mainly in the areas of oil refining, gold and copper mining, the manufacture of copra and sugar refining.

The amount of money received from the U.S. in one form or another exceeds $4,000 million and has been used mostly to reduce old debts, support the economy and finance a mutual defence force. In addition, considerable sums of money circulate as a result of American bases in the archipelago, such as Subic Bay, big enough to service the entire Seventh Fleet, and Clark Field Air Base, north of Manila, the biggest U.S. Air Force Base in the Far East. Clark Field has about 50,000 Americans and employs 27,300 local Filipinos.

Following his state visits to the United States and Japan towards the end of 1966, President Marcos reported that he had secured commitments for the financing of the country's most urgent projects obtaining nearly $45 million from the U.S. for the next four years. About $250 million would be available from Japan under the reparations agreement, while large sums would be forthcoming from the United States during the next three years to cover foreign exchange requirements. The question now is whether President Marcos can succeed where others have failed? In June 1967 a journalist in the Philippine Free Press wrote, 'Marcos's biggest problem is the erosion of his popularity and credibility among the people. Many have become disenchanted. He has lost much of his old political magic. He promised too much and has fulfilled too little'.[55]

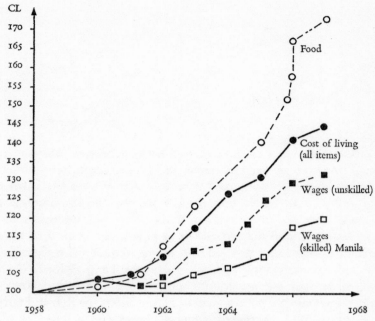

Fig 2 *Increase in Cost of Living*
Year 1958. Index = 100

10   Postscript

ALMOST TWO YEARS have elapsed since Ferdinand Marcos was
elected president of the Philippines and a new administration took
over. Looking back over 1967 it is clear that Marcos has failed to
carry out in full his election pledges to stop the importation of
rice and increase production at home, to eradicate widespread
smuggling, to avoid the imposition of new taxes or the sending of
Filipinos to Vietnam; to minimize crime, reduce unemployment,
keep food prices down and implement the Land Reform Code.
Some newspaper articles, commenting on the widespread poverty
of the masses and the ever widening gap between the rich and poor,
have sarcastically wondered whether Marcos is a Filipino. He
intervened to prevent the mayor of Manila, Antonio Villegas, from
implementing the 1954 Retail Trade Nationalization Law which
would have denied Americans the right to do retail business, and
this action caused considerable comment. Marcos maintained that
American retailers or corporations were exempt from the pro-
hibition because of parity rights, according to the Laurel-Langley
Agreement.[56] The issue was taken to the supreme court, which
decided that in matters of national policy the decisions of the
president must prevail over those of local executive officers such as
the mayor of Manila. Although Marcos won a victory, it was seen
by most people as evidence of American pressure on the president.
It was also embarrassing to Marcos because of his assurances to
American investors that conditions were favourable for them in the
Philippines.

Despite claims by the government that steps have been taken to
reduce hunger and relieve poverty among the poor, the press has

continued to print stories of social discontent and the resurgence of the rebel Huks. Extracts were printed from a report issued by a senate defence committee which stated:

The Huks are now according to the best available intelligence running a sort of 'invisible government' in Pampanga, in the western sector of Bulacan and in the southern fringes of Nueva Ecija and Tarlac. Their intensive fund raising operations have assumed scandalous proportions, underscoring the government's weak and ineffective intelligence system . . . the unholy alliance between the Huks and government officials is a downright mockery of our democratic system . . . Continuing social unrest in central Luzon reflects deteriorating economic conditions.[57]

In the senate report the Huk force was considered to be much smaller than the rebel army of the 1950s some 1,250 men with a mass support of 30,000. It was stressed that the Huks presented no threat to national security; but of course there were the intangible factors, such as the apathy of the people to national problems.

Without the support of the people the Huk movement will collapse like a house of cards. There is reason to believe that the Huk movement is in large measure an agrarian reform movement. Although the Huk leaders are either communist or have communist leanings, the rank and file of the organization is made up of poor, unschooled, landless tenants who do not know the difference between democracy and communism, they do not care a hoot what the world thinks provided that they have land of their own. In their simple minds land ownership means economic stability, independence and dignity, let alone a respectable place in the community. It is the peasant's hunger for land which is exploited by the communists.[58]

Though President Marcos dismissed parts of this report as pure exaggeration, the newspapers then disclosed that the United States had promised financial assistance and equipment to help the government fight the Huk menace. Whatever the truth of the matter, the senate report confirms, in a rather startling manner, the fundamental reasons for discontent and social unrest. Today, there is a lack of faith in congress and government which is widespread in

157

the rural areas. Even though Macapagal's controversial Land Reform Code was mutilated during its passage through congress, it would, at least, have meant a start towards reform. Since then President Marcos' administration has done little to implement the bill, as was pointed out by Macapagal in a speech before Liberal leaders in July 1967. He said, 'any claim that the Marcos administration is earnestly desirous of carrying out the land reform programme is an empty protestation'.[59] Macapagal recalled that an agreement between the United States and the Philippines in 1964 enabled the government to use part of the $28 million educational fund for land reform education. Instead, President Marcos had allocated large sums of this fund for the construction of a theatre.

Debates in congress show blatantly the failure of the Nacionalistas and Liberals to understand the vital imperatives that will enable the country to solve its many problems. One acute problem involves economic relations with the United States after the expiration of the Laurel-Langley Agreement in 1974. A number of politicians fear that an abrogation of the whole agreement would destroy all future chances of obtaining favourable trade preferences with the United States. Some American officials have not been slow to emphasize this. Other Filipinos want things to continue as hitherto and then let the Laurel-Langley Agreement and the parity question die out in 1974. Business circles are divided between those who favour a continuous trade agreement to be negotiated with the United States, and those, like the Philippine Coconut Administration (PCA), who want a change in the country's trade policy. The PCA, in particular, maintains that the Laurel-Langley Agreement is strangling the industry as a result of the diminishing tariff-free quotas. It also stresses the fact that the Philippines has failed to exploit its position as the world's single biggest supplier of coconut products. Action is needed to develop new trading partners in Europe and within the European Common Market. Many political commentators and economists warn that continued trade preferences between a country like the United States and a small undeveloped nation like the Philippines will only lead to unfortunate consequences with an increased anti-Americanism and cries of neo-colonialism.

In May 1967 the United States announced that it would provide $13 million, as an amendment to the War Damage legislation of 1962, to help the government construct some 6,000 school buildings. Almost simultaneously it was announced that President Marcos and the American Ambassador, William Blair Jr, had reached an agreement permitting the use of the Mactan airfield, Cebu, by the United States Air Force. It was strongly emphasized, however, that the base was not to be used for launching attacks on North Vietnam. This news was soon overshadowed by speculations in the press over a visit of the Indonesian Foreign Minister, Adam Malik, with the intention of promoting the formation of a regional co-operation alliance on technical and economic matters among the countries of Southeast Asia. This raised questions about the fate of ASA and Maphilindo. Since the fall of President Sukarno, diplomatic relations had been restored between Jakarta and Kuala Lumpur. The new Indonesian government hoped to form a regional association with Southeast Asian countries that would include Burma, Cambodia, Laos and Singapore in order to be prepared for the economic and political vacuum that would result if the United States should withdraw from Asia. This meant closer economic and cultural co-operation among the countries of ASA, who already had one thing in common—namely, Asian solutions for Asian problems. An important step in this direction was the formation in August 1967 of the Association of Southeast Asian Nations (ASEAN) during a meeting in Bangkok of delegations from Indonesia, Malaysia, Singapore, Thailand and the Philippines. How far these plans will progress is difficult to say, but there is no doubt that the escalation of the war in Vietnam is causing anxiety among leaders of the Southeast Asian countries. Filipinos, in particular, are worried over the involvement of the Philippines if the Vietnam conflict should develop into a major Asian war, perhaps a world war.

During the early summer of 1967 an unofficial trade mission went to Russia and countries in eastern Europe. Political commentators began to speculate whether this indicated a departure from the rigid policy of isolating the Philippines from communist countries. Speculation was kept alive by Manuel Enverga's speech to a gathering of foreign diplomats in Washington on 12 September, where he discussed the question of why the Philippines has always identified itself with the United States in its foreign relations, and why it has not maintained diplomatic and commercial ties with the communist countries? Enverga admitted these questions were both pertinent and embarrassing. For him it seemed a mistake that the Philippines had looked too much towards American help and assistance, with the result that American colonialist policies had permeated the Philippine economy and influenced its political affairs. A critical examination was now being made of both Philippine–American relations and the question of eventual relations with communist countries. For fourteen years as a member of congress he had constantly advocated the establishment of trade relations with the communist countries. He went on to say that the Philippine government was scrutinizing the defence pact with the United States, the Laurel-Langley Agreement, parity rights and the use of military bases. Enverga, who is chairman of the congress committee on foreign affairs, concluded by saying that whenever Filipinos criticized inequities or injustices in Philippine–American relations, invariably they were accused of being ungrateful. 'This we do not admit. Gratitude is one of our virtues and I ask the good people of America to try and reconsider their position.'[60]

Naturally this speech caused comment in both the United States and the Philippines, especially as Enverga had also mentioned that the Philippine congress might not sanction the future maintenance of Filipino army units in Vietnam. Did this foreshadow a radical change in Philippine foreign policy and a stop to the vacillating tactics of President Marcos over Vietnam? Such thoughts were put to one side as election fever began to spread in November, when President Marcos saw the elections as his only chance to win control of a rebellious senate, where big landowners had repeatedly blocked or diluted reform programmes. Marcos travelled some 10,000 miles around the country to persuade the electorate to vote for his Nacionalista Party candidates. Violent clashes between supporters of the rival candidates were many and more than one hundred people lost their lives during the polling. The result was a victory for Marcos and for the Nacionalista Party. Marcos could now count on a majority in both the lower and upper house of congress. Immediately after the result of the polling Marcos stated that he would carry out his pledge to make central Luzon a land reform area by 1970. He would also provide jobs for the unemployed by offering foreign investors tax-free industrial sites.[61]

Will President Marcos rise above partisan politics and carry out the essential reforms so badly needed by his country? the results of the elections leave him with little excuse. In the short time left before the presidential election in 1969 he must work hard to restore the confidence of the people. For the sake of the nation he must urge the members of both political parties to sink their differences and devote their energies to eliminating poverty, nepotism, smuggling and crime, He must de-centralize parts of the administration, free the civil service from political interference, improve transportation, communication and power facilities, and take heed of the grievances of the forgotten tribal minorities, many of whom are exploited by unscrupulous local officials and land-grabbers.

In this book I have tried to give an accurate and unbiased picture of this fascinating nation. Now I take the liberty of imploring the Philippine people to realize that the future of their country is in their own hands and not dependent on the influence of foreign countries or foreign investors, even if outside technical and financial assistance is used. In politics and public affairs they must try to curb their inability to co-operate. Highly-trained Filipinos walk the streets looking for work while senators argue incessantly over matters of little importance to the nation. The Republic of the Philippines has a form of self-government which, even if not perfect, is a model of stability compared to some other troubled and insecure countries of Southeast Asia. Many possibilities are at hand for a national effort that could be made possible by the sinking of political differences and the realization by wealthy and vested interests, that it might be better to play their part, now, in putting the Philippines on the road to prosperity rather than to take the risk of losing all they have gained sometime in the future. Such a national effort would soon show that the communist bogey and the fear of a

Chinese minority in the country are not the menace so many had been led to believe. Moreover, the Filipinos might find the national identity they are looking for and then, by their efforts and example, lead the way for a sane, united and prosperous Southeast Asia. The Philippines could have a very important future.

Notes on the Text

I THE ISLANDS AND THEIR PEOPLE

1 *Statistical Handbook of the Philippines*, Bureau of Printing, Manila, 1960.

2 Charles Robequain, *Malaya, Indonesia, Borneo and the Philippines*, London, 1959. pp. 268–272.

3 A. R. Wallace, *The Malay Archipelago*, 3rd edition, London, 1870.

4 *The Population and other Demographic facts of the Philippines*, Philippine Economy Bulletin, Vol. 11, no. 4, 1964.

5 Victor Purcell, *The Revolution in Southeast Asia*, London, 1962.

6 Excellent accounts of the minority tribes are to be found in L. Wilson, *The Skyland of the Philippines*, Baguio, 1953, and Tage Ellinger's two books, *Friend of the Brave*, Manila, 1954, and *Solen går ner i öst*, Stockholm, 1960.

2 EARLY HISTORY

7 Robert Fox, *The Philippines in Prehistoric Times*, Science Review Manila, September 1962.

8 H. Otley Beyer, *Philippine and East Asian Archaeology and its relation to the Origin of the Pacific Islands Population*, National Research Council, Bulletin no. 29, Manila, 1948.

9 R. W. Lieban, *Cebuano Sorcery*, Berkeley and Los Angeles, 1967.

10 H. Otley Beyer, *Early History of Foreign Relations with Foreign Countries, especially China*, Manila, 1948.

11 Wu Ching-hong, *A Study of References to the Philippines in Chinese Sources from Earliest Times to the Ming Dynasty*, Philippines Social Sciences and Humanities Review, Vol. XXIV, January–June, Manila, 1959.

12 E. H. Blair and J. A. Robertson, *The Philippine Islands, 1493–1898*, Vols. XXXIII–XXXIV, Cleveland, 1903–09.

13 Ibid.

163

14 Joaquin Martinez de Zuñiga, *An Historical View of the Philippine Islands*, Filipiniana Book Guild, Manila, 1966.
15 Ibid.
16 Fedor Jagor, *Reisen in den Philippinen*, Berlin, 1873.
17 Y. Mikami, *Negotiations between Hideyoshi and Dasmarinas*, Philippine Review Manila, 1916.
18 Pierre Sonnerat, *Voyage aux Indes Orientales et à la Chine*, Paris, 1772.
19 Gregorio F. Zaide, *Philippine History*, Manila, 1962.

3 THE DECLINE OF SPANISH CONTROL

20 Joaquin Martinez de Zuñiga, *An Historical View of the Philippine Islands*, Filipiniana Book Guild, Manila, 1966, and J. F. Cady, *Southeast Asia. Its Historical Development*, New York, 1964.
21 *Rizal in Retrospect*, Philippine Historical Association, Manila, 1961.
22 Najeeb M. Saleeby, *The History of Sulu*, Filipiniana Book Guild, Manila, 1963.
23 Gregorio F. Zaide, *Philippine History*, Manila, 1962.

4 AMERICAN INTERVENTION

24 Alfred Ravenholt, *The Philippines. A Young Republic on the Move*, Princeton, 1962.
25 Richard Hofstadter, *The American Political Tradition*, London, 1962.
26 J. William Fulbright, *The Arrogance of Power*, New York, 1966.
27 Onofre D. Corpuz, *The Philippines*, New Jersey, 1965.
28 An excellent account of this period is in Encarnacion Alzona, *The Origins of the Commonwealth of the Philippines*, The Commonwealth Handbook, Manila, 1936, and Joseph R. Hayden, *The Philippines, A Study in National Development*, New York, 1942.
29 Armando J. Malay, *Occupied Philippines*, Manila, 1967.
30 Headed by José Laurel, the Commission included, in addition to the members of the Executive Commission, Melecio Arranz, Emilio Aguinaldo, Manuel Briones, Vincente Madrigal, Camilo Osias, Manuel Roxas, Sultan Sa Ramain, Pedro Subido, Teofilo Sison and Miguel Unson. Ramon Avancena was appointed vice president.

5 THE BEGINNING OF FREEDOM

31 George A. Malcolm, *Pacific Affairs*, XXVII, March 1954.
32 A. V. H. Hartendorp, *History of Industry and Trade of the Philippines: The Magsaysay Administration*, Manila, 1961.

33   *Seato: 1954–1964*, Southeast Asia Treaty Organization, Bangkok, 1964.
34   Ibid.

6   THE NEW ERA

35   K. G. Tregonning, *The Claim for North Borneo by the Philippines*, Australian Outlook, XVI: 3, December 1962.
36   *Philippine Claim to Borneo*, Vol. 1, Bureau of Printing, Manila, 1964.
37   *News from the Philippines*, Dept. of Foreign Affairs, Division of Information, Series of 1966, No. 1, Manila.
38   *Philippines Free Press*, Vol. LX, no. 2, 1967.

6   SOCIETY, RELIGION AND CULTURE

39   *Philippines Free Press*, Vol. LVI, no. 2, 1963.
40   Robert Fox, 'Men and Women in the Philippines,' a chapter from *Women in the New Asia*, published UNESCO, 1965.
41   Bernabe Africa, *The Political Views of Rizal*, Philippine Historical Association, Bulletin, Vol. V, nos. 1–4, 1961.
42   *Philippines Free Press*, Vol. LX, no. 23, 1967.
43   *The Art of the Philippines: 1521–1957*, Art Association of the Philippines, Manila, 1958.
44   Lucrecia R. Kasilag, *Philippine Music: Past and Present*, UNESCO Symposium on Culture, Manila, 1961.
45   Celso Al Carunungan, *The Literature of the Filipinos*, and Leopoldo Y. Yabes, *The Literature of the Filipino Peoples*, Ibid.
46   *A Theater in Transition*, Weekly Graphic, Vol. XXXIV, no. 4, Manila, 1967.

7   GOVERNMENT, POLITICS AND EDUCATION

47   *The Philippines*, A Handbook of Information, Dept. of Foreign Affairs, Manila, 1965.
48   Manuel L. Carreon, *Emergent Nationalism in Asia*, The Philippine Economy Bulletin, NEC, Vol. 1, no. 4, Manila, 1963.
49   Sixto K. Roxas, *Investment in Education*, Ibid. Vol. 11, no. 1, Manila, 1963.

8   THE ECONOMY

50   *The Sunday Times*, London, 30 June 1968.
51   Republic of the Philippines, Republic Act 3844, *The Land Reform Code*, Manila, July 1963.

52 F. Alarcon Garde, *Foods in a Developing Economy*, The Philippine Economy Bulletin, Vol. 11, no. 5, Manila, 1964.

53 *The Philippines*, Yearbook, Far Eastern Economic Review, Hong Kong, 1967.

54 Ibid. See also, *Economic Survey of Asia and the Far East 1966*, United Nations Economic Bulletin for Asia and the Far East, Bangkok, 1967.

55 Napolean G. Rama, *The Problems of Marcos*, Philippine Free Press, Vol. LX, no. 23, Manila, 1967.

9 POSTSCRIPT

56 Republic of the Philippines, Republic Act 1355, concerning revision of the 1946 Trade agreement between the Republic of the Philippines and the United States of America, Manila, June 1955.

57 Republic of the Philippines, Senate Committee on Defense dealing with the security problems posed by a resurgence of the Huk movement. Report no. 1123. Chairman, Manuel P. Manahan. April 1967.

58 Ibid.

59 Diosdado Macapagal, *The Common Man and the Marcos Régime*, Philippine Free Press, Vol. LX, no. 30, Manila, 1967. A report of a speech before the National Directorate of the Liberal Party, July 1967.

60 Manuel S. Enverga, Vital Speeches of the Day, Vol. XXXIV, no. 1. Pelham, New York, October 1967.

61 *Philippine Elections*, New Republic, Washington, 9 December 1967.

Select Bibliography

Articles and books arranged alphabetically according to authors

Abrahamsen, Helen M., *The Philippine Islands*, Palo Alto, 1954.

Albuquerque, Affonso de, *The Commentaries of the Great Affonso D'Albuquerque, Second Viceroy of India*, Translated by Walter de Gray Birch, Hakluyt Society, London, 1875-1884.

Allen, G. C., and Donnithorne, Audrey G., *Western Enterprise in Indonesia and Malaya*, London, 1957.

Alzona, Encarnacion, 'The Origins of the Commonwealth of the Philippines',
The Philippine Commonwealth Handbook, Manila, 1936.

Araneta, Francisco S.J., 'Some Problems of Philippine Education', *Science Review*, Manila, March 1961.

Argensola, Fr. Bartolome Leonardo de, *Conquista de las Islas Malucas*, Madrid, 1609.

Aruego, Jose M., *Know Your Constitution*, Manila, 1940.

Asian Affairs, special issue on problems of economic development in Southeast Asia, 1, March 1956.

Barrantes Vincente, *Guerras piraticas de Filipinos contra Mindanao y Joloanos*, Madrid, 1879.

Bazaco, F. Evergisto, *Culture of the Early Filipinos*, University of the Philippines, Manila, 1936.

Benham, Frederic, *The Colombo Plan, and Other Essays*, London, 1956.

Benitez, Conrado, *History of the Philippines*, Boston, 1954.

Benitez, Connado and Craig, Austin, *The Philippine Progress Prior to 1898*, Manila, 1916.

Bernstein, David, *The Philippine Story*, New York, 1947.

Berreman, Gerald D., *The Philippines: A Survey of Current Social, Economic and Political Conditions*, Cornell Southeast Asia Program, Data Paper no. 19, Ithaca, 1966.

Beyer, H. Otley, 'Philippine and East Asian Archaeology and Its Relation to the Origin of the Pacific Islands Population', National Research Council, Bulletin no. 29, Manila, 1948.

Beyer, H. Otley, *Early History of Foreign Relations with Foreign Countries, Especially China*. Manila 1948.

Beyer, H. Otley, et al., *Philippine Saga: A Pictorial History of the Archipelago Since Time Began*, Manila, 1957.

Blair, E. H. and Robertson, J. A., *The Philippine Islands, 1493-1898*, 55 vols. Cleveland, Ohio, 1903-1909.

Blount, James H., *The American Occupation of the Philippines*, New York, 1912.

Blumentritt, Ferdinand, *Versuch einer Ethnographie der Philippinen*, Gotha, 1882.

Bowring, John, *A Visit to the Philippine Islands, 1858*, Filipiniana Book Guild, Manila, 1963.

Buss, Claude A., *The Far East*, New York, 1955.

Cady, J. F., *Southeast Asia; Its Historical Development*, New York, 1964.

Carreon, Manuel L., 'Emergent Nationalism in Asia', *The Philippine Economy Bulletin*, National Economic Council, Manila, March-April, 1963.

Carunungan, Celso Al, 'The Literature of the Filipinos', *UNESCO Symposium on Culture*, Manila, February, 1961.

Chronicle Yearbook, *The Philippines and the Filipnos*, Manila, 1961. pp. 30-43.

Clements, F. W., 'The World Health Organization in Southern Asia and the Western Pacific', *Pacific Affairs*, no. 25, 1952, pp. 334-348.

Cavanna y Monso, Jesus Maria, *Rizal and the Philippines of His Day*, Manila, 1957.

Corpuz, Onofre D., *The Philippines*, New Jersey, 1965.

Costa, Horacio de la, 'History and Philippine Culture', *Science Review*, Manila, May 1961; *The Jesuits in the Philippines, 1581–1768*, Cambridge, Mass. 1961.

Co Tui, Frank, 'Science in the Phillipines: A Review and a Forecast', *Fukien Times Yearbook*, Manila, 1963.

Cressey, George B., *Asia's Lands and Peoples*, New York, 1963.

Crucillo, Cornelio V., 'The Progress of Technical Cooperation in Foreign Aid Programs', *The Philippine Economy Bulletin*, Manila, March-April 1964.

Cuaderno, M., 'The Bell Trade Act and the Philippine Economy', *Pacific Affairs*, no. 25, 1952, pp 323-33.

Cuarderno, Miguel, *The Framing of the Constitution of the Philippines*, Manila, 1937.

168

Curshall, Alden, 'Tobacco production in the Philippines', Transactions of the Illinois State Academy of Science, Vol. 52, nos 1 and 2, 1959.

Dewey, George, *Autobiography of George Dewey, Admiral of the Navy*, New York, 1913.

Economic Bulletin for Asia and the Far East, United Nations, Department of Economic Affairs, Bangkok, (quarterly).

Economic survey of Asia and the Far East, United Nations, Department of Economic Affairs, Bangkok, (annual).

Ellinger, Tage U. H., *Friend of the Brave*, Manila, 1954.

Elliot, Charles B., *The Philippines to the End of the Military Régime*, Indianapolis, 1917.

Elsbree, William H., *Japan's Role in Southeast Asian Nationalist Movements, 1940–1945*, Cambridge, Mass., 1953.

Emerson, Rupert; Mills, Lennox A.; and Thompson, Virginia: *Government and Nationalism in Southeast Asia*, New York, 1942.

Emerson, Rupert, *Representative Government in Southeast Asia*, Cambridge, Mass. 1955.

Facts about the Philippines and Journal of Philippine Statistics, Vol. 14, no. 1, January-March 1961.

Far Eastern Quarterly, Special numbers: 'Southeast Asia', Nov., 1942: 'The Philippines', Feb., 1945.

Fernandez, Perfecto V., 'The Spirit of Democratic Law in the Philippines', *Fukien Times Yearbook*, Manila, 1963.

Fernando, Enrique and Africa, José L., 'Chances for the Survival of Democracy in the Philippines', Bulletin of the Institute of Pacific Relations, Manila, 1950.

Foreman, John, *The Philippine Islands*, New York, 1899.

Forbes, W. C., *The Philippine Islands*, 2nd ed. Cambridge, Mass., 1945.

Fox, Robert B., 'The Philippines in Prehistoric Times', *Science Review*, Manila, September 1962.

Funston, Frederick, *Memories of Two Wars; Cuban and Philippine Experiences*, New York, 1914.

Garbell, M. A. *Tropical and Equatorial Meteorology*, London, 1947.

Garde, F. Alarcon, 'Foods in a Developing Economy', *The Philippine Economy Bulletin*, National Economic Council, May-June 1964.

Garcia, Dominador F., 'The Philippine Constabulary and Law and Order in the Philippines', *Fukien Times Yearbook*, Manila, 1963.

Garcia, Paulino J., 'Technology Geared to National Progress', *Science Review*, Manila, March 1961.

Gironiére, Paul P. de la, *Twenty Years in the Philippines*, Filipiniana Book Guild, Manila, 1962.

Golay, Frank H.: 'Economic Consequences of the Philippine Trade Act', *Pacific Affairs*, no. 28, 1955; The Philippine Monetary Policy Debate', P.A. 29. 1956; *The Philippines: Public Policy and National Development*, Ithaca, New York, 1961.

Gordon, Bernard K., *The Dimensions of Conflict in Southeast Asia*, Princeton, New Jersey, 1966.

Gourou, P., *The Tropical World*, Trans. E. D. Laborde, London, 1953.

Grimes, A., 'The Journey of Fa-hsien from Ceylon to Canton', *Journal of the Royal Asiatic Society*, Singapore, XIX, 1941.

Griswold, Alfred W., *The Far Eastern Policy of the United States*, New York, 1938.

Grunder, Garel A., and Livezey, W. E., *The Philippines and the United States*, University of Oklahoma Press, 1951.

Handbook of Philippine Statistics, 1903–1959, Manila, 1960.

Hall, D. G., *A History of South-East Asia*, London, 1964.

Hassell, Elizabeth L., *The Sri-Vijayan and Majapahit Empires and the Theory of their Political Association with the Philippine Islands*, M.A. Thesis, University of the Philippines, 1952.

Hayden, Joseph Ralston, *The Philippines: a Study in National Development*, New York, 1942.

Higgins, Benjamin, 'Development problems in the Philippines: a comparison with Indonesia', *Far Eastern Survey*, no. 26, 1957.

Jacoby Erich, *Agrarian Unrest in Southeast Asia*, New York, 1949.

Jagor, Fedor, *Reisen in den Philippinen*, Berlin, 1873.

Jenkins, Shirley, 'Financial and Economic planning in the Philippines', *Pacific Affairs*, No. 21, 1948.

Kahin George McTurnan, *Governments and Politics of Southeast Asia*, Ithaca, New York, 1959.

Kalaw, Maximo M., *The Filipino Rebel*, Filipiniana Book Guild, Manila, 1964.

Kalaw, Teodoro M, *The Philippine Revolution*, Manila, 1925.

Kasilag, Lucrecia R., 'Philippine Music: Past and Present', *UNESCO Symposium on Culture*, Manila, February 1961.

Keesing, Felix M., *The Philippines: A Nation in the Making*, Shanghai, 1937; 'Cultural trends in the Philippines', *Far Eastern Quarterly*, no. 4, 1945.

Kolb, A., *Die Philippinen*, Leipzig, 1942.
170

Krieger, Herbert W., 'Races and Peoples in the Philippines', *Far Eastern Quarterly*, no. 4, 1945.

Kubler, George, and Martin, Soria, *Arts and Architecture in Spain and Portugal and their American Dominions*, 1500–1800, London, 1959.

Lansang, José A., 'The Philippine-American Experiment: A Filipino View', *Pacific Affairs*, no. 25, 1952.

Liang, Dapen, *Development of Philippine Political Parties*, Hongkong, 1939.

Majul, Cesar Adib, 'Islam and Arab Cultural Influences in the Philippines', *UNESCO Symposium on Culture*, Manila, February 1961.

Malcolm, George A., *The Commonwealth of the Philippines*, New York, 1936.

Martinez, Zuñiga, *Historical View of the Philippines*, Filipiniana Book Guild, Manila, 1966.

Mendinueto, S. R., 'Industrial Philippines', Congrès International de Géographie, Amsterdam, 1938.

Mikami, Y., 'Negotiations Between Hideyoshi and Dasmarinas', *Philippine Review*, Manila, 1916.

Miles, Walter K., *The Prehistory of the Philippines*, M.A. Thesis. Dept. of Anthropology, University of the Philippines, 1952.

Mills, Lennox A., *Southeast Asia*, University of Minnesota Press, 1964.

Montero y Vidal, José, *Historia general de Filipinas*, Manila, 1888.

Morga, Antonio de, *Sucesos de las Islas Filipinas*, Rizal Edition, Paris, 1890.

Morgan, R., *World Sea Fisheries*, London, 1956.

Palma, Rafael, *The Pride of the Malay Race*, Tr. by R. Ozaeta, New York, 1949.

Palmer, C. E., 'Tropical Meteorology', *Quarterly Journal of the Royal Meteorological Society*, no. 78, 1952.

Panganiban, José Villa, 'Linguistic Influences in the Philippines', *UNESCO, Symposium on Culture*, Manila, February, 1961.

Pelzer, Karl J., 'Rural problems and plans for rural development in the Republic of the Philippines', 28th Study session, International Institute of Differeing Civilization, The Hague, September, 1953.

Perkins, Dexter, *Hands Off: a History of the Monroe Doctrine*, Boston, Mass., 1943.

Phelan, John L., *The Hispanization of the Philippines: Spanish Aims and Filipino Responses*, 1565–1700. Madison, Wisc., 1959.

'Presidential policy in the Philippines', *World Today*, no. 12, 1956.

Purcell, Victor: *The Chinese in South East Asia*, Oxford 1951; *The Revolution in Southeast Asia*, London, 1962.

Quirino, Carlos, 'Rizal in Retrospect', Centennial Aniversary Issue, *Bulletin of the Philippine Historical Association*, Manila, 1961.

Ravenholt, Albert, *The Philippines: A Young Republic on the Move*, Princeton, New Jersey, 1962.

Republic of the Philippines, *The Philippines: a Handbook of Information*, Dept. of Foreign Affairs, Manila, 1965.

Republic of the Philippines, *The Philippine Claim to North Borneo*, Vol. 1. Bureau of Printing, Manila, 1964.

Riehl, R., *Tropical Meteorology*, New York, 1954.

Rizal, José, *Noli me Tangere*, (Unexpurgated edition), Tr. by Jorge Bocobo, Manila, 1956; *El Filibusterismo*, (Unexpurgated edition), Tr. by Jorge Bocobo, Manila, 1957.

Robequain, Charles, *Malaya, Indonesia, Borneo and the Philippines*, Tr. by E. D. Laborde, London, 1959.

Romani, John H., *The Philippine Presidency*, Manila, 1956.

Ronall, Joachim O., 'Spanish Revival in the Philippines', Eastern World, no. 11, 1957.

Roosevelt, Theodore, *Colonial Policies of the United States*, New York, 1937.

Rosher, Wilhelm, *Spanish Colonial System*, Tr. by E. G. Bourne, New York, 1904.

Roxas, Sixto K., 'Investment in Education: The Philippine Experience', *The Philippine Economy Bulletin*, National Economic Council, Manila, September-October 1963.

Salcedo, Juan Jr., 'Philippine Science: Today and Tomorrow', *Fukien Times Yearbook*, Manila, September, 1962.

Saleeby, N. M., *The History of Sulu*, Filipiniana Book Guild, Manila, 1963.

Santos-Cuyugan, R., 'The Changing Philippines: a Problem of Cultural Identity', *Chronicle Yearbook*, Manila, 1961.

Scaff, Alvin H., *The Philippine Answer to Communism*, Stanford, Cal., 1955.

Schurz, William Lytle, *The Manila Galleon*, New York, 1939.

Scott-Smith, Winfield, ed., *Arts of the Philippines*. Art Association of the Philippines, Manila, 1958.

Smith, R. A., *Philippine Freedom, 1946–1958*, New York, 1958.

Smith, W. G., *Geology and Mineral Resources of the Philippine Islands*, Manila, 1924.

Spencer, J. E., *Land and People in the Philippines*, Berkeley and Los Angeles, Cal, 1954.

Stephens, Robert P., 'The Prospect for Social Progress in the Philippines', *Pacific Affairs*, no. 23, 1950.

Tregonning, K. G., 'The Claim to North Borneo by the Philippines', *Australian Outlook*, XVI: 3, December, 1962.

UNESCO. Proceedings of the Symposium on Typhoons, Tokyo, 1954.

United Nations: Report of the Ministerial Conference on Asian Economic Cooperation, ECAFE, Bangkok, January, 1964; 'Population Growth and Manpower in the Philippines', *Population Studies*, no. 32, New York, 1960; *Statistical Yearbook*.

United States, Department of War: Reports of the Philippine Commission, the Civil Governor and the Heads of the Executive Depts., Civil Government of the Philippine Islands, 1900–1903. Washington D.C. 1904.

Unger, L., 'The Chinese in Southeast Asia', *Geographical Review*, no. 34, 1944.

Virchow, Rudolf, *The Peopling of the Philippines*. Translated from German, Smithsonian Institute, Washington D.C., 1899.

Wallace, A. R., *The Malay Archipelago*, 3rd edition, London, 1872.

Wernstedt, Frederick: *The role and importance of Philippine inter-island shipping and trade*, Cornell S.E. Asia Programme, Data paper no. 26, Ithaca, New York, 1957; 'Cebu: focus of Philippine inter-island trade', *Economic Geography*, 1957.

Wheatley, Paul, 'The Malay Peninsula as Known to the Chinese of the Third Century A.D.', *Journal of the Royal Asiatic Society*, no. 28, 1955.

Wilson, Laurence Lee, The Skyland of the Philippines. Baguio, 1953.

Wolfstone, Daniel, 'Manila's image of Asia', *Far Eastern Economic Review*, September, 1960.

Worcester, Dean Conant, and Hayden, Ralston, *The Philippines: Past and Present*, New York, 1914 and 1930.

Wu Ching-hong, 'A Study of References to the Philippines in Chinese Sources from Earliest Times to the Ming Dynasty', *Philippine Social Sciences and Humanities Review*, January–June, 1959.

Yabes, Leopoldo Y., 'The Literature of the Filipino Peoples', *UNESCO Symposium on Culture*, Manila, February 1961.

Zaide, Gregorio F.: *Philippine Political and Cultural History*, Manila, 1953; *Philippine History*, Manila, 1962.

Acknowledgements

Photographs taken by the author, 12, 13, 14, 15, 16, 17, 18, 19, 21, 22, 25, 33, 35; J. T. de Bry and J. L. de Bry: *Ander Theil der Orientalischen Indien*, 1958, 1; T. de Bry: *Das vierdte Buch von der neuwen Welt*, 1613, 4; Camera Press, 10, 11, 27, 36; J. Allan Cash, 20, 32, 34; L. Choris: *Voyage pittoresque autour du monde*, 1822, 2; *Illustration Filipina*, 1859, 3; Imperial War Museum, 8; *Philippine Magazine*, 1899, 7; Philippine Tourist and Travel Assoc., 23, 28, 30, 31; Paul Popper Ltd. 26, 29; Gaspar de San Agustan: *Conquistas des las Ilas Philippinas*, 1698, 5; Unicef, 24; Fig. 1, ECAFE Bulletin for Asia, Vol. XVII 1966/67.

Who's Who

AGUINALDO, EMILIO (1869–1964). Leader of the Katipunan after Bonifacio's death in 1897. Following the United States occupation of the Philippines, he formed the first Philippine Republic at Malolos; but he was soon captured and retired to private life. He was later accused of collaboration with the Japanese and imprisoned by U.S. officials. President Quirino appointed him member of the council of state in 1950.

ALONTO, DOMOCAO (b. 1914). Son of the Sultan and Bai (Princess) Bariga Alangadi, of the powerful Lanao family who strongly influenced the Muslims. He was a guerrilla fighter during the Second World War and elected to the Senate in 1955 as a Nacionalista.

AMORSOLO, FERNANDO (b. 1892). The 'grand old man' of Philippine painters, he attracted attention by 1920 as an illustrator and painter. His impressionist style and bold use of colour has considerably influenced Filipino painting. By the 1930s Amorsolo had established a widespread following and today his influence is seen in the work of most traditional painters.

ANDA, SIMON DE (died 1776). As governor-general of the Philippines between 1770–76 he launched an attack on the interference of friars in civil affairs. As a judge of the royal *Audencia* Anda had resisted the British occupation of Manila during the Seven Year's War.

AQUINO, MELCHORA (1812–1919). A woman patriot who helped the Katipunan in their rebellion against Spanish rule, after their first declaration at Balintawak, Rizal. She is known as Tandang Sora, 'Mother of Balintawak'. The Spanish governor exiled her to Guam, where she remained until the U.S. occupation.

175

BALTAZAR, FRANCISCO (1788–1862). The first Filipino to win prominence as a Tagalog writer with his epic romance *Florante at Laura*. He is called the 'Prince of Tagalog Poets', and is also known as Balagtas.

BARRERA, JESUS (b. 1896). Prominent lawyer and an under-secretary of justice in the Magsaysay administration. As an active member of the Civil Liberties Union he has championed the cause of the poor and the tenant farmers. He is a member of the Nacionalista Party.

BENITEZ, CONRADO (b. 1889). Distinguished educator, economist and historian and former member of the National Economic Council. He was one of the Committee of Seven which drafted the Philippine Constitution in 1934, and is an employer delegate to the International Labour Organization.

BONIFACIO, ANDRES (1863–1897). Revolutionary leader who created and organized the Katipunan. On 26 August 1896 he gave the signal for a countrywide revolt. He was self-educated and profoundly influenced by Rizal's novels and the French Revolution. Executed at Mount Buntis by revolutionary faction supported by Aguinaldo.

BURGOS, JOSÉ (1837–1872). Filipino priest who fought for the cause of the people against Spanish rule. Accused of complicity in the Cavite mutiny, he was executed with two other priests, Gomez and Zamora.

CASTILLO, ANDRES V. (b. 1903). An economist and adviser to the Philippine government, appointed in 1962 as Governor of the Central Bank by President Macapagal.

CUADERNO, MIGUEL SR. (b. 1890). A distinguished soldier, lawyer, banker, economist and adviser to Philippine presidents. He was a member of the committee which presented the Commonwealth Constitution to President Roosevelt for signature. In 1948 he was appointed Governor of the Central Bank.

DAGOHOY, FRANCISCO (18th c.). Filipino patriot. In 1774 he incited a rebellion in Bohol against Spanish friars, which took the Spanish fifty years to control. He also established a form of free government in the mountains.

176

DEWEY, GEORGE (1837–1917). Commodore of the U.S. naval squadron which destroyed the Spanish fleet in Manila Bay in 1898.

GARCIA, CARLOS POLESTICO (b. 1896). President of the Philippines between 1957 and 1961. He played an important part in the formation and development of SEATO.

GOMEZ, MARIANO (1799–1872). A priest of Bacoor who founded the newspaper *La Verdad*, which exposed Spanish abuses. He was branded as a radical and executed with Burgos and Zamora.

JACINTO, EMILIO (1875–1899). Intellectual leader of the Katipunan. Like Bonifacio he had come from a poor merchant family and was able by education to overcome his poverty. He became Bonifacio's adviser and wrote the revolutionary documents of the Katipunan.

KALANTIAW, RAJAH (15th c.). The third chief of Panay in pre-Spanish times. He set down a code of justice and is often referred to historically as the Filipino lawmaker. The Kalantiaw Code covered many subjects such as family relations, property rights, adoption, divorce, contracts, crimes and even laziness.

KIRAM, RAJA MUDA ADMIRUL (1868–1949?). The former Sultan of Sulu. Following the U.S. occupation, Kiram, known as Kiram II, concluded a treaty to establish amicable relations with the United States and define the status of the Sulu Sultanate. This agreement, known as the 'Bates Agreement', recognized American sovereignty over Sulu. It was first approved by President McKinley but later abrogated by Congress.

LAPU-LAPU (16th c.). The first Filipino to defy the Spaniards in 1521. Chief of the small island of Mactan, outside of Cebu, he refused to become a Christian and accept Spanish sovereignty. He successfully defied Magellan in a battle in which the Spanish leader was killed.

LACSON, ARSENIO H. (1912–1962). A lawyer, journalist, radio commentator and politician. He first won recognition as a fearless guerrilla fighter during the Japanese occupation. Subsequently exposed the corruption in the Philippine government and the excesses of the United States Army in Palawan and Olongapo. He was offered various bribes to keep

O

silent and was banned from broadcasting in 1947. After being elected to Congress in 1949, he resigned two years later to run as the Nacionalista candidate for Mayor of Manila, which he won by a large majority.

LAUREL, JOSÉ P. (1891–1959). A prominent educator, writer and lawyer who was President of the Philippines during the Japanese occupation. He later became a Senator and Judge of the Supreme Court.

LEGAZPI, MIGUEL LOPEZ DE (died 1572). The first governor of the Philippines. He is often called the Conqueror of the Philippines, and he initiated the Spanish conquest of the archipelago.

LIM, VINCENTE (1888–1945). Soldier. The first Filipino to be graduated from the U.S. Military Academy at West Point, N.Y., and to be commissioned in the U.S army. He later organized the Commonwealth army. During World War II he was an active guerrilla fighter and later executed by the Japanese for refusing to reveal secret information.

LOPEZ, EUGENIO (b. 1901). Head of a powerful family with controlling interests in broadcasting, cement, shipping, sugar, insurance, and publishing companies. Lopez and his brother Fernando, were charged by President Macapagal in 1963 with using their power to control the political and economic life of the nation. In reply the Lopezes accused Macapagal of harassment and persecution.

LOPEZ, SALVADOR P. (b. 1911). Distinguished writer, diplomat, politician. He was the Philippines permanent representative to the United Nations (1953–54) and later Ambassador to France. As Under-Secretary of Foreign Affairs in 1962–63 he attracted attention because of his pro-Indonesian policies. Because of the need for a change of policy in 1963, he served for only six months as Secretary of Foreign Affairs.

LUNA, ANTONIO (1866–1899). A doctor of pharmacology, a brilliant writer and revolutionary leader who opposed the U.S. occupation of the Philippines. He was a member of the propagandists in Europe and had a short imprisonment in Spain. Though an excellent soldier, he was a poor politician and was murdered by his countrymen. He was the younger brother of Juan Luna.

LUNA, JUAN (1857–1899). The first Filipine painter to win international recognition. He studied under Alejo Vera in Spain, where he combined painting with assistance to the propaganda movement. In 1881 Luna won the first prize at the Madrid Exposition with a massive canvas entitled *Spoliarium*. Returning to the Philippines he was arrested for spreading anti-Spanish propaganda. After his release Juan went to Hong-Kong, where he died.

MABINI, APOLINARIO (1864–1903). Prominent patriot and philosopher of the revolutionary period. Shortly after the proclamation of independence Mabini became the chief adviser to General Aguinaldo. He is considered the brains behind the creation of the provisional republic at Malolos.

MACAPAGAL, DIOSDADO (b. 1910). President of the Philippines between 1961–65. He was the son of a poor tenant farmer, and was influenced by Magsaysay's ideas and reforms. As president he announced a programme of land reform and encouraged the production of raw materials and Philippine industries. He supported Indonesia and disagreed with the U.S. In spite of his reforms, the economic situation remained underdeveloped. In 1965 he was succeeded by Ferdinand Marcos.

MAGELLAN, FERDINAND (1480–1521) A Portuguese sailor and explorer who in service to the Spanish crown was the first to reach the Spice Islands from the west across the Pacific and to discover the Philippines. He was killed when trying to suppress Lapu-lapu on the island of Mactan.

MAGSAYSAY, RAMON (1907–1957). President of the Philippines between 1953–57. During Japanese occupation he had been a prominent guerrilla leader; and because of his success in appeasing the Hukbalahap movement he was made secretary of defence by President Quirino in 1950. As presiden the introduced the controversial Agricultural Tenancy Act and thereby helped to break the Hukbalahap revolt. To encourage reforms he supported emerging middle-class leaders and challenged the corrupt practices of the ruling élite. At the height of his popularity he was killed in an air crash on Mt. Manungal, Cebu.

MARCOS, E. FERDINAND (b. 1917). President of the Philippines since 1965. During World War II he distinguished himself as a guerrilla fighter and an intelligence officer. In 1949 he was elected to congress and in 1959 he became a senator. He disagreed with President Macapagal's Indonesian policy and in 1964 resigned as leader of the Liberal Party. Almost immediately the Nacionalista Party nominated him as their presidential candidate.

MERRITT, WESLEY (1836–1910). Distinguished American soldier who commanded the United States forces sent to the Philippines after Dewey's victory in 1898. He was the first military governor of the Philippines for a brief period and then member of the delegation which negotiated the settlement of the Spanish-American War.

OSMEÑA, SERGIO SR. (1878–1961). Statesman and the first leader of the Nacionalista Party. Following a split among the Nacionalistas and the establishment of the Coalition Party Osmeña was elected as Vice-President of the Philippines in 1935. After the Japanese occupation, he went to the U.S. to serve the government in exile. In 1944 he became President following Quezon's death but two years later he was defeated by Manuel Roxas.

PALMA, JOSÉ (1876–1903). Soldier, poet and patriot during the revolutionary period. Wrote the poem *Filipinas* to the march composed by Julian Felipe which became the Philippine National Hymn.

PALMA, RAFAEL (1874–1939). Writer, lawyer, statesman and educator. He was appointed President of the University of the Philippines in 1925. He was the author of a controversial biography of Rizal published in 1949. An abridged edition of this book was published in English—*Pride of the Malay Race*, translated by Roman Ozaeta.

PATERNO, A. PEDRO (1857–1911). A prominent lawyer, writer and poet. His first poems, written in Spanish, were published in Madrid in 1880 under the title *Sampaguitas Y. Poesias Varias*. During the revolutionary period he acted as a peacemaker between the Spanish authorities and the Filipinos. He negotiated the Pact of Biaknabato between General Primo de Rivera and Emilio Aguinaldo in 1897. He was president of the Congress of the Revolutionary Government which drafted a constitution of the first Philippine Republic. After the fall of Malolos, Paterno considered resistance to the Americans as useless and he worked with the

Taft Commission to bring about peace. He helped to establish the first political party in the Philippines, the Federal Party, which collaborated with the United States. In 1911 his *Synopsis de Historia de Filipinas* was published.

PELAEZ, EMMANUEL (b. 1915). A prominent politician known for his support of scientific research and economic development. Former foreign affairs secretary and a supporter of southeast Asian cooperation.

PILAR, GREGORIO DEL (1875–1899). A student at the Ateneo de Manila when the revolution broke out and the youngest general among the revolutionary heros. In command of Aguinaldo's bodyguard, he was killed in the Battle of Tirad Pass in 1899.

PILAR, MARCELO DEL (1850–1896). In 1882 he founded the first daily newspaper published in the Tagalog text. A writer who exposed abuses committed by the Spanish regime. Compelled to flee to Spain in 1888 because of anti-friar documents, he took charge of *La Solidaridad,* the newspaper of the Filipino propagandists. He died in poverty in Barcelona.

PONCE, MARIANO (1863–1918). A revolutionary and active member of the propagandists, who tried to get Japanese support for the Filipinos. He was a friend of Rizal's.

QUEZON, LUIS MANUEL (1878–1944). President of the Philippines between 1935 and 1944. As a student he studied law and later joined the revolutionary forces as a soldier. In 1906 with Osmeña and others he founded the Immediate Independence Party which became the Nationalist Party. He was elected to the Assembly and in 1916 he was elected President of the Philippine Senate. In 1933 he led a delegation to the U.S. which won support for the Tydings-McDuffie Act, which provided for a Philippine constitutional convention, national elections and the establishment of a Commonwealth government. In 1935 Quezon was elected president and proved to be a dynamic leader who promoted social justice. Following the Japanese invasion he set up government in exile in the U.S., where he died in 1944.

QUIRINO, ELPIDIO (1890–1956). The second president of the Republic of the Philippines. He had studied law and was a member of the mission to the United States that obtained the passage of the Tydings-McDuffie Act in 1934. He was elected to the Senate in 1941. During the Japanese occupation he remained in the Philippines and after the liberation he joined the government as secretary of finance in the Roxas administration. Two months later when the Republic was established he became Vice-President and Secretary of Foreign Affairs. In 1949 he succeeded Roxas. As President he took active steps to foster foreign relations. A peace treaty was signed with Japan and in 1951 a mutual defence agreement was concluded with the United States. In 1953 he was defeated by Magsaysay in the presidential election.

RECTO, CLARO M. (1890–1960). A lawyer, satirist, politician and justice of the Supreme Court. He is also the author of many books about politics and law. He was president of the constitutional convention that drafted the Philippine Constitution in 1934. First elected to the Senate in 1931 he was elected a number of times both as the Nacionalista and Liberal candidate. Recto represented the Philippines in the International Court of Justice at Hague.

RIZAL, JOSÉ (1861–1896). Doctor, linguist, novelist and propagandist. He was the most gifted of Filipino polemicists and gave inspiration to Philippine nationalism. His two novels, *Noli me Tangere* and *Filibusterismo*, exposed the evils of Spanish rule and were widely read. In July 1892 he founded the Liga Filipina which immediately aroused the suspicions of the Spaniards and within a few days he was arrested and exiled to Dapitan, on the northern shore of Mindanao. Here he settled down to other interests and reportedly kept aloof from political activity. In 1893 to vindicate himself he offered his services as a doctor to the Spanish army in Cuba. While waiting to leave for Cuba in August 1896 he became involved in the revolt which broke out following the Spaniards' discovery of the Katipunan. Disassociating himself from this uprising he was able to leave Manila for Spain, but on his arrival he was arrested and sent back to the Philippines to stand trial for the incitement of rebellion. On 30 December 1896, he was executed.

RODRIQUEZ, EULOGIO, SR. (1883–1964). Financial tycoon and civic leader known as Amang the Commoner. Perennial President of the Nacionalista party which he brought back to power by undermining the Liberal regime under President Quirino. Elected to the Senate in 1941.

ROMULO, CARLOS P. (b. 1899). A diplomat, publisher, author, soldier and former President of the United Nations General Assembly. Well known outside of the Philippines, Romulo was the first Filipino to win the American Pulitzer Prize in Journalism in 1941. He was president of the University of the Philippines and was Minister of Education between 1966–68.

ROXAS, MANUEL (1892–1948). A lawyer, orator and politician, who served under General Douglas MacArthur during World War II. After the liberation he came into conflict with the returning President Osmeña and in 1945 left the Nacionalista party to found the Liberal party. With the tacit support of MacArthur he contested the Commonwealth presidential election held in April 1946 and successfully defeated Osmeña. Shortly afterwards he became the first president of the Philippine Republic. His efforts to ensure the smooth passage of the Parity Amendments to the Constitution, which among other things accorded equal rights to American citizens until 1974, met with strong criticism and he narrowly escaped assassination in March, 1947. Roxas died while delivering a speech at Clark Field, the U.S. airbase in April, 1948.

SANTOS, LOPE K. (1879–1963). A poet and statesman who helped to organize the first Nacionalista party. He has been the foremost exponent of the use of Tagalog as the national language. Director of the National Language Institute.

SOLIMAN, RAJAH (16th c.). The recognized Moslem ruler of Maynilad, now Manila, and the grandson of Lakan Dula, ruler of the adjoining Tondo. He refused to submit to vassalage following the arrival of the Spanish forces led by Legazpi in 1571. Alleged to have been killed during an attack against the Spaniards. His name has been linked with a person called Agustin de Legazpi, who was executed by the Spanish in 1588 on charges of conspiracy.

URDUJA, PRINCESS (13th c.). Legendary ruler of a kingdom which is now Pangasinan. She was famous as a warrior and remained unmarried because she insisted that her husband be braver, stronger and wiser than herself.

YULO, JOSÉ (b. 1894). A landowner, lawyer, economist and adviser to four Philippine presidents. Appointed Secretary of Justice by Governor Murphy in 1934 and during the Japanese occupation served as Chief Justice of the Supreme Court. As an active member of the Liberal Party, in 1953 he was a candidate for the vice-presidency. In 1957 he was the Liberal candidate for the presidency. On both occasions he was defeated by Carlos P. Garcia. Yulo still plays a leading role in politics.

ZAMORA JACINTO (1835–1872) Parochial priest of Pasig. Together with two other priests, Burgos and Gomez, he was accused of plotting against the Spanish following the Cavite revolt and executed in 1872.

Index

Numbers in italics refer to illustrations

DATE DUE

14

Demco, Inc. 38-293